INCESTUOUS FAMILIES

I hear the cries of pain,
The silence that speaks of grief
And wonder,
        Can they ever find relief?
I feel their disbelief and sadness
And see their lovelessness
And wonder,
        What is the answer to their pain?
To see this human havoc
        is pain enough.
To be that person
        must be terribly tough.
To know these brave survivors
        is to see their strength,
A shimmering diamond,
        shining bright.

*From a poem by Jan Lincecum MacLean.

INCESTUOUS FAMILIES

By

GEORGE THORMAN, M.A., M.S.W.

Professor of Social Work
St. Edward's University
Austin, Texas

CHARLES C THOMAS • PUBLISHER
Springfield • Illinois • U.S.A.

Published and Distributed Throughout the World by

CHARLES C THOMAS • PUBLISHER
2600 South First Street
Springfield, Illinois, 62717, U.S.A.

This book is protected by copyright. No part of it
may be reproduced in any manner without written
permission from the publisher.

© *1983 by* CHARLES C THOMAS • PUBLISHER

ISBN 0-398-04808-8

Library of Congress Catalog Card Number: 82-19476

With THOMAS BOOKS *careful attention is given to all details of
manufacturing and design. It is the Publisher's desire to present books that
are satisfactory as to their physical qualities and artistic possibilities and
appropriate for their particular use. THOMAS BOOKS will be true to those
laws of quality that assure a good name and good will.*

Printed in the United States of America

I-R-1

Library of Congress Cataloging in Publication Data

Thorman, George.
    Incestuous families.

    Bibliography: p.
    Includes index.
        1. Incest.   2. Child molesting.   3. Child abuse.
4. Mentally ill – Family relationships.   I. Title.
[DNLM: 1. Incest. WM 610 T495i]
RC560.I53T46   1983   616.85'83   82-19476
ISBN 0-398-04808-8

PREFACE

INCEST is a closely guarded family secret protected by a conspiracy of silence between the offender and the victim. Mar-
garet Mead points out that our culture considers sex relations
between close family members to be an "unthinkable abomina-
tion." So strong is the incest taboo that the thought of fathers
sexually abusing their daughters, mothers seducing their sons and
brothers sexually exploiting their sisters is inherently repugnant.
Many people believe that incest rarely, if ever, occurs in a civilized
society, but studies indicate that incest is found at all social levels
and affects the lives of as many as twenty million Americans. It is
estimated that the number of children who are sexually abused
equals or exceeds the number of children who are physically
abused by their parents.

This book is designed to provide concerned citizens with an
overview of the nature, extent and effects of incest and to serve
as a resource for professional persons who seek a greater understanding of the treatment and prevention of sexual abuse within
the family. I have a strong conviction that the family plays a crucial role in the development of the person. As Nathan Ackerman
pointed out, "The emotional give and take of family relationships
is the crucial center of forces that make or break mental health."
Because incest represents a serious problem of disturbed family
relations, social workers and other helping professionals have a
special concern about family sexual abuse of children.

Formal research on incest is quite limited, and much of what
is known about the causes and effects of incestuous relationships
has been acquired from the personal accounts of incest victims and
from the reports of professional persons to whom they have
turned for help. Incest victims who have broken the barrier of

silence and spoken out have provided a clearer understanding of
the problems that they have had to face. I have made extensive
use of these personal accounts to provide a vivid picture of how incest develops and to describe the trauma involved in an incestuous
experience. The case studies included in this book have been derived from the work of psychologists, social workers, psychiatrists
and social scientists who have devoted their efforts to developing effective methods of intervention in families when incest
occurs.

Chapter One provides an overview of incest, the origin of the
taboo against sexual relations between family members and the
purpose that the taboo serves in maintaining the family as a viable
social institution. Common misconceptions about incest are examined, and various types of sexual misuse of children by family
members are described, including father-daughter, mother-son and
other incestuous relations. Chapter Two outlines the dynamics of
father-daughter incest and describes how the relation between these
two family members develops into a sexual liaison and how it is
maintained by the father's promises, threats and bribes. This
chapter also examines why the father uses the daughter as the
object of his sexual attention and inquires into the role that the
mother plays in the development of the incestuous tie. The
process of victimization of the daughter and the effects of disclosure are also described.

Chapter Three includes an examination of the factors that produce incest in certain family systems with special reference to
those specific characteristics that are found in most incestuous
families. Attention is focused on how barriers in communication
contribute to the problems these families face, and the role of the
victim as family scapegoat is described. Chapter Four outlines
the steps in the treatment of incestuous families and the techniques of intervention employed to bring about change within
the family system. Various approaches to helping are also described, and the effect of stress is pointed to as a contributing
factor in the development of incest. The roles of the various helping professions in working with incestuous families are described
and differentiated. The appropriate use of individual therapy,
group therapy and family therapy as intervention strategies is dis-

cussed.

Chapter Five is an examination into the use of the legal system in cases of sexual abuse of children by family members. The nature of the legal process is discussed in regard to the need to protect the child from sexual abuse and to provide a safe environment that will serve the best interest of the incest victim. Alternatives to criminal prosecution of the incest offender are examined, and programs designed to rehabilitate the family are described. Chapter Six includes an examination of the impact of incest on the victim as an adult, the emotional trauma that results and the sexual problems that victims often face. Also included is a discussion of the various approaches that help victims cope with anger and feelings of distrust that they carry into adult life because they were betrayed by those who were thought to be loving, caring persons.

Chapter Seven explores measures that can be taken to reduce the incidence of incest. Included is a description of the warning signs that indicate incest may be taking place, the use of crisis intervention in stopping sexual abuse and recommendations for reducing stress that impairs family functioning. The need for an intensive research program to study the causes of incest and to develop more effective treatment methods is emphasized. In conclusion, the need to modify existing institutions that perpetuate incest by supporting the partriarchal family system is considered as an effective approach to the prevention of incest.

To assist me in gaining insight into the impact of incest on the lives of those who have been sexually abused by family members, I called upon Jan MacLean and Tom Burditt, who have been working with victims and their families at the Austin Child Guidance and Evaluation Center. Jan shared her experience in forming a support group for women who survived the incest experience. Her professional knowledge of the impact of incest helped me appreciate the importance of helping those who bear the scars of sexual abuse. Tom's experience in working with offenders and their families helped me understand the psychodynamics of incest and the treatment of incestuous behavior.

I am deeply indebted to those women who volunteered to talk with me about their personal experiences as incest victims. Their contribution to my understanding of the long-term con-

sequences of an incestuous relationship is most sincerely appreciated. The testimony of these women brings to light the shame, the
guilt and the anger that lingers far into adult life. I salute them for
having the courage to speak out, and I applaud them for their
ability to survive the abuse and trauma they have undergone.

G.T.

CONTENTS

INCESTUOUS FAMILIES

Chapter 1

THE INCEST TABOO

My mother went into the hospital for a nervous breakdown when I was about seven years old. I was supposed to stay with neighbors, but my dad would make me come home to make dinner and visit. All I wanted was my mother. I missed her so much that even the house and the furniture seemed physically different without her. Once in a while my father would make me stay overnight with him. He'd have me sit by him and would tell me how much he needed me. That was when he began touching me sexually. I didn't really mind it at first. I was so alone and needed the attention and the contact so badly that I wanted him to touch me.

In the beginning, I would wake up just as he was leaving my room at night. I wouldn't really know what had just happened. Then I would wake up with his hands on me or just before he came into the room. Later, I got so I would wake up just before his car drove into the driveway. I lived in a constant state of waiting, never knowing when he would come into my room.

At first, he would just stand by the bed and touch me. Later, he began to lay in the bed beside me. Although he began by being gentle, as time went on he became rougher and rougher. He would leave me feeling sore and bruised for days. It was as if he completely lost touch with the fact that I was a child.

Total detachment became my way of dealing with what went on at night. I would roll into the wall when he came in, pretending to be asleep, trying to become part of the wall.

3

> I would cry hysterically in order to get so far into my
> own pain that I wouldn't notice what he was doing. With
> the pillow over my face, I taught myself to detach my
> mind from my body. I could actually see myself from the
> far corner of the room: I saw the little girl crying in bed.
> And I felt sorry for her.
>
>   Barbara L. Myers

BARBARA Myers, the woman who gave this account of her incestuous experience, is one of an estimated 10-20 million women who have been victims of incest. Authorities point out that incest is the most common form of sexual abuse and that it is also the least often reported. The full nature and extent of incest is unknown because of underreporting and lack of reliable statistics on a national basis, but studies indicate that one out of every four females will be sexually abused in some way before she reaches the age of eighteen. In 75 percent of the cases, the victim knows her assailant, and in 34 percent, the sexual molestation happens in her home.

Each year hundreds of thousands of children and adolescents are sexually abused. The American Humane Society estimates that the rate of sexual abuse is 40 per 1,000,000 in the United States. The National Center on Child Abuse currently sets the annual incidence of sexual abuse of children at over 100,000 cases each year.[1]

Sexual abuse of children is not a new problem or a rare occurrence. It is not easily identified, and because it rarely results in physical injury, it goes undetected and is not reported to authorities. Sexual abuse can be defined as contacts or interactions between an adult and a child when the victim is being used to gratify the adult's needs and desires. Much of this maltreatment of children and adolescents in the family takes place within the child's own home. Recent studies show that out of 9,000 cases of sex crimes against children, 75 percent could be traced to members of the victim's household, to relatives, neighbors or acquaintances. Half of all offenders were family members. Some studies indicate that parents, stepparents, substitute parents or relatives are involved in as high as 80 percent of all cases. A 1977 study concludes that about one in ten persons have been involved in an incestuous experience at some point in their lives, and according to David Walter the number of persons who become victims of incest may go as high as a quarter of a million cases each year.[2]

The number of cases of incestuous relationships actually reported to authorities represents only the tip of the iceberg. Neither the victim nor the victim's family is usually inclined to disclose and report incest. Adult family members bring pressure to bear on the child not to reveal the situation to anyone outside the family. Social workers find that daughters are the most reluctant to reveal that they have had sex relations with their fathers because they will be accused of seducing him by their provocative appearance and behavior. Some feel that they must remain silent because disclosure would not only disgrace them and the family but also would end in the arrest and imprisonment of their fathers. Disclosure often threatens to destroy the family, and the daughter often feels it necessary to remain silent to prevent this possibility.

The following statement was made by a thirty-one-year-old victim who promised not to reveal her sexual relationship with her father so as to prevent him from molesting her stepsister: "I find myself, an adult thirty-one years old, still trying to come to grips with the devastating effect that it has had on my life . . . I have a long history of deceit. Since I was a little ten-year-old child I had to deceive the world and my mother; that my father took a sexual interest in me and initiated sexual activities with me."[3] In some cases, the victim feels trapped because no one would believe her if she revealed the facts. A thirty-seven-year-old woman explained her reason for not disclosing that her father made a sexual assault on her as a child: "He started messing with me for the first time when we were out camping. I ran out of the tent and started running around the lake as fast as I could. There was nobody up there, so I thought to myself, Who am I going to tell? Especially, since it was my father, who was going to believe me? So I slowly walked back to the tent. What else could I do?"[4] Once her father was certain that the daughter would not reveal what had happened, he felt free to continue the sexual exploitation of his daughter.

Myths about Incest

Because it is a very strong taboo, many myths have grown up

around where, how and why incest occurs. Contrary to common belief, incest is not limited to certain geographic regions and social classes. The hill people of Appalachia and the poor people in America are not the only groups that commit incest. "Incest is relentlessly democratic," writes Sandra Butler. Her view is borne out by the Santa Clara California Treatment Center where a study of 400 families referred to the program indicated that incest included a broad spectrum of occupations, incomes and racial compositions. The fathers were engaged in professional, semiprofessional, skilled and blue-collar occupations. The average income of these families was close to that of other families living in the county, and no group was disproportionately represented.[5] Yet many people assume that incest will never happen in their own families or in the families of their neighbors or friends. This mistaken attitude is a major obstacle to dealing with the problem of incest because it fosters the secrecy and isolaton that are the very basis for the continuation of incestuous relationships.

In some cases, the incestuous relationship has been hidden by the victim and is later discovered inadvertently. A school nurse who talked with a student who refused to undress for gym class was shocked to find that the child was an incest victim. "When she told me that she wouldn't undress in gym, I was suspicious," she said. "Then she showed me the marks on her breasts. If it hadn't been for the gym situation coming up, we might never have known. She was so quiet, we just thought she was introverted."

Contrary to popular belief, incest is not a one- or two-time occurrence in the life of the victim. Studies indicate that the typical incest relationship has been going on for at least two years before it is discovered. Cases of children experiencing incest with their fathers as early as two or three years of age and continuing into the teen years are not uncommon. A thirty-two-year-old past victim recalled that the first incestual assault with her father occurred when she was age three and continued until age six, at which time her mother left her father. The mother remarried when the daughter was age seven. She remembered that her stepfather misused her sexually most of the time. As a teenager she felt that she was tainted, "that something was wrong with me forever!" A twenty-year-old past victim recounts that she was seven when the first sexual encounter with her father took place. The incest continued until she was twelve years of age. "There was a time in my life when my father would coerce sex from me at least once a week," she recalled. "It is almost unnecessary to say that I gave up fighting. I would hide. I would hate it, but somehow I couldn't run away from home, as I so often wanted to do."

Many people assume that a child who is the victim of incest has been forced to submit to a sexual relationship through acts of violence and rape. On the contrary, the father rarely uses physical force to gain access to his daughter. The child usually cooperates because the father offers rewards, promises, special favors, or gives the victim special attention that is not accorded to other persons in the family. However, there is evidence that suggests a trend toward an increased use of force and violence in the sexual abuse of children by family members. The offender can effectively use threats to frighten the child and gain compliance with his wishes. Intimidation is often used to force the child to submit to sexual advances. Even though the child is not subjected to acts of physical cruelty, the psychological effects are quite damaging.

Subtle forms of pressure are exerted to gain access to the young child. The father may tell the child that he is acting in her best interest by teaching her the "facts of life," and that she will not have to find out what sex is all about from a stranger. Some fathers tell the child that "there is nothing wrong about what we are doing" and then warn that dire consequences will follow if others learn about the sex games they are playing. The insistence on secrecy leaves the child in a state of confusion. As one victim put it: "I couldn't understand why I couldn't tell my mother what my father was doing if it really wasn't wrong." She continued, "Whenever I would tell him to stop because what we were doing was wrong, he kept telling that what we were doing wasn't like grown up, married love. He'd tell me he loved me too much for that."

It is often assumed that sexual involvement with a family member is less harmful than sexual relations with a stranger because the parent loves the child. The fact that incest occurs in the context of a caring relationship makes the experience more traumatic because the trust placed in the parent is betrayed. The victim grows up distrusting adults, especially men. The long-term consequences often appear when the young adult woman tries to form a satisfactory relationship with men and finds it extremely difficult to overcome her early sex experiences with her father. As Louise Armstrong points out, the violation of the daughter by the father is quite different from the experience of being raped. "Rape by a stranger is quick and brutal. It allows for a straight-forward reaction — anger, hate," she writes. "But the seduction or coercion of a child by a needed and trusted parent is far more complex."[6] Follow-up studies of adults who were victimized by their fathers bear out this conclusion. Incest is often hazardous to mental health. Psychiatrists report that as many as 20-30 percent of the disturbed children that they see in clinics have been victims of incest, and mental health experts believe that only one out of four females involved in incest has suffered no serious ill effects.

There is a widely accepted belief that the victim of incest invites sexual advances from the offender. The daughter, it is argued, turns her father on in order to gain some personal advantage. Some people believe that girls are naturally seductive and adept at the art of involving their fathers in an incestuous relationship. Some children do have active sex fantasies. Adults can use these fantasies and turn them into sexual relationships. The responsibility for incest rests with the parents in any case. As Sanford points out: "In exceedingly rare cases little girls do ask their fathers to fondle their genitals," she writes. "Even if they do, it is the adult's responsibility to assess the short- and long-term potential harm. It is the father's responsibility not to do it." Sanford also points out that the daughter who becomes involved in a sexual relationship is really seeking affection from her father rather than a sexual liaison with him. "Little girls seeking affection, attention or favor from their fathers with 'niceness' are definitely not asking an adult to throw his better judgment to the wind and sexually exploit them," Sanford concludes.

Associated with the notion that girls are seductive is the idea that the victim of incest actually enjoys the experience. There is some evidence that pleasure is derived in a few instances, but there is usually much more pain than enjoyment involved in incest. Most accounts clearly express revulsion. A thirty-six-year-old past victim recalls her feelings: "I remember him taking his pants down and saying 'come over here' and sitting on the bed. And I remember a feeling of total fear, total revulsion. I knew somehow it was perverse. I remember being frightened and acutely uncomfortable." A twenty-year-old past victim describes her experience:

> The older I got, the more he wanted to penetrate, and then I would say no. But I just couldn't get away from it. There was no way I could escape it. I didn't want it. I did not want him to bother me. It was just something my father wanted. I wouldn't allow myself to feel. He would do whatever he wanted. I would just cry during the whole time and say, 'I hate you. Leave me alone. I hate you, I hate you, I hate you.' I would cry and scream and he would say, 'Shut up, shut up.' And he would do it until he was satisfied.

The view that the mother is responsible for permitting an incest situation to develop because she chooses to ignore or deny that it is happening is widely accepted. But most mothers do not know that the daughter is being victimized by the father because he has threatened her and sworn her to absolute secrecy. In some cases, the mother may suspect what is happening without the daughter directly telling her the facts. If the mother confronts the father, the daughter and the father may strongly deny that they are carrying on an incestuous relation. A mother who was herself a victim of incest did attempt to intervene but was unsuccessful in stopping it. She stated: "I did say something to him. Asked him point blank. I had gone through that as a kid, and no kid of mine was going to. Of couse he denied it, but what was worse was that my daughter denied it too. She stood up for him. Later I found out he had threatened her, but then it was all too weird. What could I do under the circumstances?"

Mothers are sometimes blamed for the father turning to the daughter for sexual fulfillment because the wife is cold and sexually unresponsive. The father often uses this as an excuse to explain his behavior and tells his daughter that he needs her attention and love because her mother has rejected him. The daughter is apt to accept her father's version of what is happening in the marriage even though she is not capable of knowing why her parents are having problems. "I never understood why he needed me sexually," said a nineteen-year-old past victim. "My mother slept with him every night. But he said she rejected him, so he needed me. If she had been there for him, the incest probably would not have happened." Many incestuous fathers are having an active sex life with their wives and at the same time are sexually exploiting their daughters. Incest is not a simple matter of sexual dissatisfaction in the marriage. The role of the mother in incest is quite complex; she cannot be held totally responsible for the fact that her husband initiates sex with the daughter.

Placing the blame for incest on mothers and wives can easily divert attention from the fact that society has a responsibility to refuse to sanction incest under any and all circumstances. The myth that mothers are responsible perpetuates the view that intervention from outside the family is not needed. What is essential to prevent incest? Louise Armstrong points out that incest can only happen in secret. Breaking open the secret is therefore the most effective way to prevent father-daughter incest from occurring. The difficulty in breaking through the wall of secrecy that surrounds incest can be traced to the fact that most women are dependent on men for survival. Their dependecy on men makes it possible for fathers to seduce and exploit their daughters because the mother and the daughter are both in a sense victims of their dependence on the father. Therefore, they are afraid to speak out when incest occurs, are extremely reluctant to talk about even the possibility of incest and in some instances may close their eyes to what is actually happening. The secrecy is reinforced by the social attitude that incest is disgraceful and that it does not happen in "nice" families. The conspiracy of silence is therefore solidified, and the daughter continues to be sexually exploited. "Generation after generation of women have learned that you don't talk about things like that," says Armstrong. "The most reassuring thought that I have is that if society refuses to sanction incest, breaking the secret may break down the incidence."

What Is Incest?

Definitions of incest vary from one culture to another. Behavior that is considered to be incestuous in one society may be regarded as nonincestuous in another. In some societies, sexual intimacy between family members is not considered incest and is actually encouraged. The Kalanga of Java have a tradition that sexual relations between sons and mothers will insure prosperity. Among the Yakuts of Siberia, it is considered bad luck if a girl is married as a virgin, and her brothers take her virginity from her in order to bring good fortune to her and her family. Among the Indians of the Sierra Madre mountains in Mexico, father-daughter incest is still found to exist.

In contrast, some soceites strictly forbid sex between family members, and rules of avoidance prohibit contact between them in order to guard against the possibility that incest will occur. On the Gazelle Peninsula in New Britain, a woman may no longer speak to her brother after she is married. Among the Akamba in British East Africa, a girl must carefully avoid contact with her father between the time she reaches puberty and her marriage. Among some primitive peoples, the incest taboo is strictly enforced and the usual penalty is death. Such harsh penalties are imposed because violations are thought to bring about great disasters. The inhabitants of the Gilbert Islands believe that if incest went unpunished, the sun would fall from the sky. On the Celebes Islands in Indonesia, incest was believed to cause crop failure, and on the Mindando islands in the Philippines, it was believed to be responsible for floods. According to anthropologists, the primitive belief that sex relations between family members was certain to cause a disaster was handed down from one generation to the next and eventually was accepted as a rule governing sexual behavior.

Sociological View of Incest

Sociologists have speculated about the purpose that the incest taboo serves. One sociologist, A.D. Coult, is credited with having developed the theory that the incest taboo defines and differentiates roles within the family. By so doing, it imposes order on the family system. R.E.L. Masters agrees with this "role strain theory," pointing out that the family would be disrupted if members had free sexual access to one another. "Sexual rivalries, with consequent hatreds, would spring up in some cases," he writes. "Roles within the family would be confused and discipline would be difficult, if not impossible, to enforce. The always precarious harmony of the family unit could not survive the tension." Sociologist Talcott Parsons suggests that the incest taboo serves an important role in the socialization of the individual, because it forces children to leave the family of origin and establish their own families. Sons and daughters must look to someone outside their immediate family to gratify their sexual and affectional needs. If the taboo did not exist, children would remain tied to their parents and would not be forced to become autonomous adults. The incest taboo breaks the emotional and sexual ties between children and parents. The children are forced to move out of a close symbiotic relationship with their parents and assume the role of responsible adults.

Freudian View of Incest

According to Freud, the incest taboo prevents the family members from carrying out unconscious sexual desires that would create serious problems for the family. He suggests that sons have a strong sexual desire to possess their mothers, and that daughters have sexual feelings toward their fathers. Therefore, sons would try to replace their fathers and daughters would try to replace their mothers were it not for the restraining force of the incest taboo. The incest taboo holds powerful forces of hostility and conflict in control by establishing the authority of the father over the sexual life of the family. It empowers him to punish the son if he tries to possess the mother. Therefore, the son fears the father because he can inflict the ultimate penalty for incest — castration. It follows that the incest taboo also gives the father control over the women in the family. Once he has achieved this special status, the father begins to view his wife and his daughters as property to do with as he chooses. He sees his daughters as sexual objects and assumes the right to use them to meet his sexual needs.

In her book, *Against Our Will*, Susan Brownmiller describes the mentality that the incestuous father develops. "The taboo against father rape is superceded by a stronger, possibly older taboo — there shall be no outside interference in the absolute dictatorship of the father rule," she writes.[7] This view that the daughter is the sexual property of the father tends to weaken the taboo against father-daughter incest, and although he enforces the prohibition against mother-son incest, he violates the rule against sex between father and daughter. This accounts for the fact that father-daughter incest occurs more frequently than mother-son incest and explains why girls far outnumber boys as victims of incest.

A Feminist View of Incest

A feminist analysis of father-daughter incest suggests that, because the incest taboo reinforces the absolute right of the father in the family, it is part and parcel of a patriarchal social structure that oppresses women. Firestone emphasizes that the father provides material support for the wife who in turn provides sexual services for him, and that he regards the children who are the product of this sexual union as his legal property. She writes: "His rights over them are complete. If he is not a kind father/master, tough luck. They cannot escape his clutches until they are grown."[8] Schein noted that girls grow up in this oppressive situation and therefore sense that the father is powerful and the mother is powerless. They also learn that the father's love and approval is given to those who comply with his wishes. The power of the father sets the stage for incest. Herman and Hirschman observe that the incest taboo is at the center of attempts that men make to control warfare among themselves. In a patriarchal society, women are regarded as possessions of men. The incest taboo is an agreement among men as to how women will be shared. By restricting access to certain women in the family, the incest taboo sets the rules that determine how males will settle their differences.[9] McIntyre argues that incestuous assaults enforce the dominance of the male and are another form of violence against women and children inherent in relationships promoted by partriarchy.[10] Because women are powerless in a patriarchal society, Susan Butler claims that "we need to look at women's oppression as a direct cause of incestuous assault."[11]

Legal Definitions of Incest

Incest is defined by law as sexual intercourse between persons who are closely related, the most common form being parents who have sex with their children. Some forms of intra-family

sex are not included in legal definitions of incest but have some of
the same features. For example, a man may have sex with his
stepdaughters, and, because they are not related to him by blood
ties, this type of relationship does not usually fall within the legal
limits of incest. Nevertheless, the child is sexually exploited by
an adult who is in the role of a parent and is therefore someone
who has the same psychological meaning as if he were the child's
biological parent.

The legal definitions and procedures relating to incest vary
from state to state. Most legal definitions include only those sexual acts between family members that result in penetration as falling within the limits of incest. Many laws make reference to what
was actually done to the child. The age of the victim and relationship to the perpetrator are also taken into account in many states.
Furthermore, an act of sexual abuse committed by a person outside the family may be defined and handled quite differently than
a situation in which the same act is committed by a person who is
legally responsible for the child. As with other forms of child
abuse, there is general agreement concerning the most extreme
cases, but what specific behaviors constitute incest remains largely
a matter of jurisdictional and individual interpretation. Many
terms used to describe incest are interchangeable and add to the
nebulous way in which legal and nonlegal definitions of incest are
framed.

In 1978 the United States Congress amended the Child Abuse
Prevention and Treatment Act of 1974 to include within the definition of child abuse and neglect "sexual abuse or exploitation
by a person who is responsible for the child's welfare." Some
states define incest as a form of child abuse rather than a criminal
act and deal with it in the same manner as cases involving physical
abuse of children by their parents. This broader definition of incest is consistent with scientific thinking on the problem of intra-
family sexuality. Many authorities consider any form of sexual
activity between parent and child or brother and sister to be
included in the general category of incest and regard incest as a
continuing activity rather than a single act.

The National Center on Child Abuse and Neglect uses the term
intra-family sexual abuse as a synonym for incest and defines that
form of sexual abuse as any act "perpetrated on a child by a

member of that child's family group." The definition includes not only sexual intercourse, but "any act designed to stimulate a child sexually or to use a child for the sexual stimulation, either of the perpetrator or of another person." The purpose of this definition of incest is to underscore the need to protect children from sexual maltreatment rather than to set forth specific kinds of behavior that are prohibited or that fall within the definition of incest as sexual intercourse between child and parent.

Incest may involve family members in a variety of ways. Most cases that are referred for legal investigation appear to be sexual offenses committed by fathers against their daughters. Mother-son incest is rarely reported, perhaps because of the special stigma that is attached to sex relations between mother and son. Brother-sister incest is believed to be quite common but is usually reported only if the brother is considerably older than the sister. Incest also occurs in extended family relationships and sometimes involves grandparents or uncles. If the relationship between the child and extended family members is maintained over a fairly long period of time, the relationship is usually considered incestuous.

Father-Daughter Incest

Father-daughter incest is the most frequently reported form of incestuous behavior. Such cases may involve the daughter's biological father, the mother's boyfriend or the girl's stepfather or other male figure that plays the role of male authority in the life of the female child or the adolescent girl. In some families, the incestuous behavior is limited to one particular daughter. Frequently, the oldest daughter is the one who becomes involved as in this case of a thirty-nine-year-old man who carried on a sexual relationship with his fourteen-year-old daughter over a period of two years. He began having sexual relationships with her after his wife deserted him and described her as the one who initiated the relation by offering herself in place of her mother. The sexual behavior began with the daughter masturbating the father and progressed to performing oral sex and later to sexual intercourse. Although there were other female children in the family, the father did not become involved with them or with anyone else during the two years that he was having sex with his daughter.

In this case, the daughter acted in the role of wife and sexual partner in the absence of her mother. In some families, the husband is looking for a source of emotional support that he lacks from his wife. Sometimes the wife feels abandoned by the husband emotionally, turns elsewhere for companionship and becomes indifferent to her husband. The husband then looks to his daughter to play the role of wife-mother. In such cases, the father-daughter incest frequently begins after the emotional and sexual ties between the parents have deteriorated as illustrated in the case of a man who made sexual advances on his adopted daughter when she was eleven years old. The girl's parents had slept in separate rooms, and sexual relations had been reduced to once or twice per year. The father said that he was crushed when he discovered that his wife was having an affair and threatened to leave. At this point, he turned to his daughter for affection and sexual gratification.

In most cases, sexual contact begins with exhibitionism, fondling and masturbation extending over a period of months or even years. Intercourse is usually not attempted until the girl has reached puberty. The first encounter between father and daughter usually takes place when she is about nine years old. Cases have been reported that involve a daughter who is less than one year old, but these are very rare. Some daughters become involved after they have reached puberty and may continue in the relationship into late-teen years. One clinical report based on a study of fifteen victims of father-daughter incest found that the majority of the women were the oldest or only daughters in the family and were between the ages of six and nine when they were first approached to engage in sexual behavior with their fathers. The youngest girl was four years old at the time and the oldest was fourteen. The women reported that the sexual contacts usually took place repeatedly and in most cases lasted over a period of three years or more. Physical force was not used, and intercourse was rarely attempted until the girl had reached puberty. Sexual contact was limited to masturbation and fondling the girl's breast and genital areas. In all but two of these fifteen cases, sexual relationships between daughter and father remained secret, and there was no intervention by authorities to terminate the relationship.

The Incestuous Fathers

Various studies of fathers who become involved in sexual relationships with their daughters or stepdaughters have led to the tentative conclusion that certain personality traits are found in these men. Gebhard and his associates at the Kinsey Sex Institute found that fathers who commit incest with children under age twelve were typically ineffectual, nonaggressive and drank heavily. They were preoccupied with sex, liked mouth-genital contact, preferred a variety of positions in sexual intercourse, lengthy foreplay and engaged in extramarital sex. These fathers had a poor relationship with their parents and came from unstable and unhappy homes.[12]

Fathers who became involved in a sexual relationship with their daughters at a later period in the child's life, from age twelve to age fifteen, were too diverse and nondescript to differentiate as to personality traits. However, the use of alcohol appeared to play an important part in precipitating the sexual encounter with the daughters in this group of incestuous fathers.

Fathers who became sexually involved wth their daughters over sixteen years of age were from large families, and their relationships with their parents were satisfactory. They grew up in a strict moral atmosphere during adolescence, were moralistic, conservative and religiously devout. In their middle thirties, these fathers began to take an interest in oral sex and extramarital affairs. They had poor impulse control and came from families where morality was publicly upheld but was not practiced in private. These incestuous fathers made distinctions that were used to justify their sexual relationships with their daughters. The following statement from one daughter is illustrative: "During the entire time my father was having me masturbate and fellate him, he would give all of us daughters long lectures about being virgins when we got married because of our religion. He did everything to me but penetrate."

Weinberg distinguishes between several types of incestuous fathers: *endogamic, indiscriminately promiscuous,* and *pedophilic.*[13] The endogamic father limits his sexual interests and activities to members of his immediate family because he does not cultivate social or sexual contacts with women outside the family. Therefore, he resorts to sex with his daughter to fill his need for sexual gratification. Those who are sexually promiscuous are often psychopathic individuals who have little sense of guilt or responsibility for their behavior and engage in sexual activities indiscriminately with a number of persons both inside and outside the family. For example, a twenty-year-old divorced father was arrested for raping his fifteen-year-old brother. At age thirteen, he had become sexually active with males, and at age seventeen he became sexually involved with an older woman and then with a girl his own age. He married her, and two years later he began to force his twelve-year-old sister to have intercourse with him in the presence of his wife. Following sex with his sister, he would than have intercourse with his wife. In some cases, this type of father will become violent, sadistic, and inflict physical pain on the daughter with whom he is having sexual relations.

The pedophile is an adult who has sexual fantasies about children and carries out sexual acts with them. The fathers in this group are marginal or inadequate individuals who are overwhelmed by the demands of life. Some pedophilic fathers originally preferred adult sex partners, but when faced with stress, they regress to immature forms of sexual behavior. If they encounter a difficulty or undergo a stressful situation, they become depressed. An incestuous relationship with a young daughter seems to relieve the stress and depression. At the same time that they are having sex with their daughters, these men are also actively involved in sex with their wives. A twenty-six-year-old father explained why he became involved in an incestuous relation with his five-year-old daughter in order to resolve his difficulties. "Whenever things were bad at the factory, all I had to do was think of Lisa," he said. "She spent all her time at home with me. Even at age five she could make me feel better. She was the only person I ever looked forward to seeing."

Even though they appear to others as competent and successful individuals, many incestuous fathers suffer from a poor self-image and lack confidence in their relationship to adult women. Geiser provides this explanation of how they often turn ·

to a daughter for the renewal of self-confidence.

> The fear of rejection from adult women provides some insight into why such a man may turn to his daughters. He is usually confident that the child will not reject him. The daughter usually sees her father as wonderful and great. She doesn't challenge or question him and is often initially flattered by the attention. This dynamic has been described as looking for the "youth connection." With the child's natural submission to the authority of the parent, the incestuous situation is one in which the father can count on being in control.[14]

Sanford points out that when a father feels inadequate, rejected or overwhelmed he begins to look to the daughter as the person who is most easily available to fill his needs. Sometimes the father sees in his daughter the person that his wife was when the marriage was new. "It is as though the father is taking a trip down memory lane," writes Sanford. "In this emotional time-machine, the father is not necessarily perceiving his daughter as another adult. It is more likely that he perceives himself as much younger than he actually is. He and his daughter become the same age in some purgatory between adulthood and childhood. In contrast, the mother may be seen as the "big, bad adult."

The Daughters in Incestuous Families

Many daughters who become involved in incest suffer from feelings of low self-esteem and a lack of self-confidence, which plays an important part in their sexual relationships with their fathers. A girl who feels inadequate may welcome the attention that she receives from her father as compensation for her feelings of unworthiness, even at the price of becoming involved with him sexually. The incestuous father also uses this need for acceptance and love as a powerful influence over the daughter, realizing that she is looking to him for fulfillment of important emotional needs. This basic need for love and affection can be easily exploited. Susan Forward quotes a patient who was a former victim of incest as saying: "We were all starved in our family — not for food, we always had plenty of money — but for feelings. Nobody ever seemed to feel anything. At least when I had sex with my father, I could feel something."

Daughters who get involved in an incestuous relationship appear to have negative feelings toward their mothers and ambivalent or positive feelings toward their fathers. Studies of incestuous families referred to a child guidance center reported that the girls often saw their mothers as cruel, unjust and depriving persons. "These girls had long felt abandoned by the mother as a protective adult," writes Kaufman. "In contrast, all the victims seem to have some warm feelings toward their fathers and describe them in much more favorable terms than their mothers."[15] In a study of adult women who had been involved in a sexual relationship with their fathers as children, Herman and Hirschman found that "though these women were sometimes expressing disappointment and even contempt for their fathers, they did not feel as keenly the sense of betrayal as they felt towards their mothers. Having abandoned the hope of pleasing their mothers, they seemed relieved to have found some way of pleasing their fathers and gaining their attention."[16] The study also indicated that, even though the victims felt they were powerless and helpless against their fathers, their special relation also put them in a position of some semblance of power within the family. They often assumed the role of the surrogate mother and the many responsibilities that she usually carried out. They also gained authority over younger children in the family and had a special relationship with the father that their siblings envied. Even though they resented being sexually exploited, they did feel important in the role they were given. Many girls said they felt an enormous sense of responsibility for holding the family together, and they also knew that as keepers of the incest secret, they had the power to destroy the family by revealing the incestuous relationship. "Their sexual contact with their fathers conferred on them a sense of possessing a dangerous, secret power over the lives of others, power derived from no other source."

Mothers in Incestuous Families

Most studies of incest indicate a disturbed and even hostile relationship between mother and daughter. The estrangement between them is present prior to the development of the sexual relationship with the father and often involves a displacement of the mother by the daughter. In some cases, the mother becomes incapacitated by a physical or mental illness, and it falls to the daughter to carry out the daily routine of caring for the family. The daughters then perceive their mothers as persons who are weak, dependent and ineffectual. In other cases, the rift between the mother and daughter is expressed in open hostility, and in some instances the daughter feels that she has been emotionally abandoned by the mother.

Based on their own survey of incestuous families, Blair and Rita Justice found that role reversal between mother and daughter was one of the most frequent characteristics in incestuous relationships. "The mother wants to become the child and the child wants to become the mother," they observe. "This basic symbiotic quality is reflected in nearly all the characteristics of the mothers whose husbands and daughters engage in incest."[17] As the mother turns over many of her role functions to the daughter, the possibility of a sexual involvement with the father is increased, according to this view. The mothers are perceived as inadequate to perform their duties as the nurturing persons in the family, and the daughter then begins to supply the father with the emotional support that is not forthcoming from his wife.

The Justices also concluded that the mothers in incestuous families are frigid or want no sex with their husbands. This lack of sexual interest leads to dissatisfaction on the part of the husband who then turns to the daughter for sexual fulfillment. In other respects, the Justices conclude, the mother abandons her role and invites the daughter to take over. She keeps herself tired and is in a chronic state of fatigue that makes it impossible for her to carry out her sexual and nurturing role, or she is weak and submissive, feels completely dependent on her husband and is afraid to assert herself. Her dependency and nonassertive personality prevent her from taking steps to protect her daughter from incest. "If a showdown comes and she must choose between her husband and her daughter, she will choose her husband," write the Justices. "This mother views her husband as her prime source of security, if not care and comfort, and she will do almost anything not to lose him."

Commenting on the passivity and dependence of the mothers

in incestuous families, Meiselman points out that in some cases the father is "overcontrolling, emotionally cold, and even physically abusive in a manner that verges on sadism. We then assume that the woman must be extremely dependent on her husband and tend to attribute immaturity to her since her dependency needs exceed the normal adult, even for women." Meiselman points out that mothers are expected to protect their children from any and all forms of abuse. "If she does not restrain the father in an incest situation, she is seen as having failed in a very important aspect of her maternal role."

Greenberg noted that blaming wives and mothers for the incest that husbands and fathers commit is similar to blaming the victims of incest for seducing the fathers. McIntyre also objects to "sexist assumptions" that form the basis for blaming the mother rather than the offender for the sexual assault on the daughter. "Mothers do not contribute to incest because of some psychoanalytical, formulated personality characteristics or because they cannot or do not fulfill their traditional roles of wife and mother," he writes. "Although family systems may by no means function harmoniously, the assault was performed by the perpetrator — no one else." McIntyre concludes that the root cause of incest is the patriarchal nature of the social structure: "The reality is clear. Patriarchal culture and male dominance set the stage for incest to occur."

The various views represented by these studies of incestuous families indicate that no one cause or explanation is totally adequate or valid in all respects. As we begin to take a comprehensive view of the incestuous family as compared to normal, healthy families, the reasons for the development of incest in certain family systems will be clarified. In Chapter Three, such an analysis will be made.

Other Types of Incest

Father-daughter incest is the most frequently reported and acknowledged form of intra-family sex. Other types of incestuous relations that have been known to practitioners and researchers include mother-son incest, brother-sister incest and incest with extended family members such as uncles, aunts and grandparents.

Mother-Son Incest

On the basis of known cases, mothers commit incest less frequently than other family members. In a 1955 study of 203 incestuous families, Weinberg found only two instances of mother-son relations, and the Justices found only two cases among the 112 families included in their survey. Probably 95 percent of all mother-son cases of incest are found in families without fathers or in households where the father is absent for extended periods. The absence of the father may sometimes cause the mother to seek a substitute person who will fill her need for companionship and affection. She looks to her son to fulfill this need for emotional gratification and eventually the relationship between mother and son may become highly intimate and seductive.

Three basic patterns of mother-son incest have been described by professionals who have been consulted to treat such cases. The first type involves a very low level of sexual contact. Mother and son sleep together, dress and undress together and perhaps bathe together. Sexual intercourse is rarely involved. Although the mother usually regards this relationship as completely innocent, the son may be sexually stimulated by such intimate contacts with her. If the son continues to sleep with the mother, becomes her social escort and moves in to the role of husband, the relationship becomes tinged with highly erotic feelings and fantasies. The consequences may be damaging to the son as he becomes overly attached to the mother, is socially isolated and sexually frustrated.

The second form of mother-son incest is more directly sexual in character. When the son is young, the mother bathes him. After he is older, the mother may stimulate the son's penis in the process of bathing him. When he reaches puberty, she may masturbate him to ejaculation. The son derives sexual pleasure from the mother's seductive behavior, finds it erotically stimulating and exciting. However, he is frustrated by the limitations placed on the sexual relationship with the mother because she limits her sexual activity to fondling his genitals or exposing her body. Although the mother's behavior implies some sexual payoff to the son, very rarely does she actually fulfill a promise of sexual gratification through intercourse. Mother-son incest has been romanticized in literature and often regarded as noninjurious to the son. However, this is not the case. Masters and Johnson conclude that this form of incest is injurious and results in creating serious problems in sexual adjustment for the son in adult life.

Brother-Sister Incest

Some experts in the field of sexual behavior estimate that sexual contact between siblings occurs in one family out of ten and believe that various forms of sexual interaction between brother and sister are very widespread. This type of behavior is quite harmless and natural when young siblings are about the same age. During early childhood, brothers and sisters are quite sexually naive and frequently play the game, "show me yours and I'll show you mine." These sexual contacts are innocent forms of sex education. However, if the brother is considerably older than the sister, the behavior takes on a different connotation and is usually considered to be incestuous in nature. Complex psychological factors enter into the desire for the older brother to involve the sister in a sexual relationship. Studies indicate that incest then becomes a means of coping with unconscious needs and conflicts. The older brother may have been intimidated by women and dominated by an overly aggressive mother, then takes out this hostility toward her by sexually abusing his younger sister.

Sometimes the sexual abuse results in rape as illustrated in the case of a victim who was admitted to the hospital after a suicide attempt. The woman recalled that her mother had encouraged her to sleep with her sixteen-year-old brother when she was only five years old. There were repeated instances of sexual assault by the brother. After he raped her, the sister finally revealed the facts to her mother and the incestuous relationship ended. But the impact lived on. "After that I withdrew a lot," she told her therapist. "I never had a lot of friends because I was afraid to bring them home, but after my brother raped me I couldn't face anyone. I was ashamed. I didn't understand what he was doing to me, but I knew it was wrong because it hurt and he told me not to tell."

Older sisters sometimes seduce their younger brothers. Masters and Johnson cite two cases and both involved broken homes with absent fathers. In one case, the sister was seven years older than her brother. In the other case, the sister was ten years older.[18] The result of an incestuous relationship with an older sister causes serious sexual problems for the brother in adult life. The dynamics are very similar to that of incest between mother and son. When he attempts to have sexual intercourse later in his life, the sexual partner reminds him of his sister and his guilt causes him to become impotent and avoid women.

Grandfather-Granddaughter Incest

In our society, older men are thought to have lost all interest in sex, and, therefore, the likelihood of a sexual involvement of a grandfather with his granddaughter is considered to be extremely rare. However, this type of incest does occur, especially if the grandfather lives in the same household and has daily contact with the child. An older man may have difficulty adjusting to the aging process and feel that he is not as competent and powerful as he once was. When he retires, he moves in with his children. The family often treats him as if he were senile, which contributes to his feeling of inadequacy and loss of self-respect. In this state, he is in need of someone who will make him feel strong, vigorous and important. The grandchild often fills this important need if the grandfather looks to her for affection and develops a strong emotional tie to her.

The grandfather looks to the granddaughter to restore his sense of manliness, and she offers him affection and companionship. The grandfather also becomes a source of comfort and enjoyment to the granddaughter. Sometimes he takes care of her during the absence of the parents. If he is given this responsibility, he has many opportunities to develop an incestuous relationship with her and make physical contact through hugging and kissing. Eventually, the innocent displays of affection take on a sexual tone. The incestuous behavior usually takes the form of fondling the child's body or masturbation. In some cases, oral-genital contact may be part of the sexual interaction. At first, the granddaughter finds some pleasure in the sex games that she plays with her grandfather. Flattered by his attention, she may continue the relationship for some time without revealing what is happening. Once she realizes that the behavior is not appropriate, she begins to feel guilty. If she tells her parent about what is happening, they may discount her story. A twenty-year-old past victim recalled how her parents reacted when she told them about her grandfather's "sex games." When she was five, her grandfather started putting his hands between her legs underneath her pants; the granddaughter did the same thing to her brother. Her parents wanted to know how she learned to do this, and she told them about her grandfather's behavior. Her parents thought she had made up the story. They said he was too old to do anything like that.

The principal factor in motivating the grandfather to involve the granddaughter in sexual activity is loneliness, and a profound sense of isolation and uselessness. Forward and Buck point out that this form of incest, more than any other, reflects a problem that is really a social problem rather than a private one. "It is our neglectful treatment of our aged that precipitates the majority of such cases," they write. "A grandfather who is active in the family with his own interests and friends will not easily sink into the pit of helplessness and loneliness that can lead to incest."[19]

Our knowledge of intra-family sex is still quite limited. More is known about father-daughter incest than any other form of incestuous behavior. In the chapter that follows, the father-daughter relationship in incestuous families will be the focus of attention as we examine how incest begins, how family members are involved and the conditions that bring about such relationships.

REFERENCES

1. U.S. Department of Health and Human Services: *Child Sexual Abuse.* Washington, D.C., 1980.
2. Walters, D.R.: *Physical and Sexual Abuse of Children.* Bloomington, Ind., Indiana U. Press, 1975.
3. Burgess, A.W.: Divided loyalty in incest cases. In Burgess, A.W.: *Sexual Abuse of Children and Adolescents.* Lexington, Mass., D. C. Heath, 1978.
4. Sanford, L.T.: *The Silent Children.* New York, Anchor Press, 1980.
5. Giaretto, H.: Treatment of father-daughter incest. *Children Today,* July-August, 1976.
6. Armstrong, L.: *Kiss Daddy Goodnight.* New York, Pocket Books, 1979.
7. Brownmiller, S.: *Against Our Will.* New York, Simon and Schuster, 1975.
8. Firestone, S.: *The Dialectic of Sex.* New York, William R. Morrow, 1970.
9. Herman, J., and Hirschman, L.: Father-daughter incest. *Signs, 2:* 739-740, 1977.

10. McIntyre, K.: Roles of mothers in father-daughter incest. *Social Work,* 26:463, May, 1982.
11. Butler, S.: *Conspiracy of Silence.* San Francisco, New Glide Publications, 1978.
12. Gebhard, P.H.: *Sex Offenders.* New York, Harper and Row, 1965.
13. Weinberg, S.: *Incest Behavior.* Secaucus, N.J., Citadel Press, 1976.
14. Geiser, R.: *Hidden Victims.* Boston, Mass., 1981.
15. Kaufman, L.: Family constellation and overt incestuous relations between father and daughter. *Am J Orthopsychiatry, 24:* 266-279, 1954.
16. Herman, J., and Hirschman, L.: Father-daughter incest. *Signs,* 2: 739-740, 1977.
17. Justice, B., and Justice R.: *The Broken Taboo.* New York, Human Sciences Press, 1979, p. 97.
18. Masters, W., and Johnson, V.: Incest: The ultimate taboo. *Redbook,* April, 1976.
19. Forward, S., and Buck, C.: *Betrayal of Innocence.* New York, Penguin Books, 1978, p. 115.

Chapter 2

BREAKING THE INCEST TABOO

> Incest is not a true taboo —
> just a long-lived and very,
> very well-kept secret.
>
> Louise Armstrong

DURING recent years, women who are past victims of incest have broken through the wall of silence that surrounds incest and are talking about what happened to them as children and adolescents. Some were only three years old when their fathers introduced them to an incestuous relationship. Others became objects for sexual exploitation when their fathers considered them to be fair game as teenagers. Most of them have tried to wipe the experience from their memories and some have reconstructed their lives despite the trauma. All carry the scars of incest, and many have become bitter, hostile and disillusioned adults. Those who have turned to psychotherapists and social workers for help in coping with the problems that stem from a sexual relationship with their fathers present a startling, vivid picture of how incest begins, why it continues and how they attempted to break the incestuous tie.

The following account of a thirty-three-year-old divorced woman who was involved in a sexual relationship with her father from the age of nine until she reached her fifteenth birthday describes her experience during an interview with the author.

Ann's parents were divorced soon after she and her twin sister, Tammy, were born. Ann's mother, a registered nurse, worked split shifts and left the children in the care of their grandparents. For the first nine years of her life, Ann considered her grandparents to be her surrogate parents. They provided daily

28

care and affection to the young children. "Mamma never had much responsibility for raising us," Ann stated. "It wasn't Mamma who had lunch ready for us when we came home from school, and Mamma was never the one I would go to if I needed help with a problem." Ann didn't know anything about her father who was living in Virginia. "We never saw him or heard anything about him until we were nine years old," she said.

It was at this point in Ann's life that she became aware that her mother was considering a remarriage to the twins' father. Ann recalled that her mother would occasionally date men in the nearby community, but she always wanted both her daughters to accompany her on such occasions. Ann concluded that her mother was afraid she might be sexually assaulted and "took us along for some kind of protection in case she was propositioned or something." Ann and her sister, Tammy, also went with their mother when she went on her honeymoon.

The mother's decision to remarry came as a suprise to Ann and her sister. They both considered the marriage was really a matter of convenience for the mother, according to Ann. "My mother didn't really love him," she said. "I think that when my mother hit age forty, she thought she was getting old and was going nowhere. So she took a vacation, went to visit my father in Virginia and came back and told us we would have to leave our grandparents and go to live with her and Daddy in Virginia." The move was a painful experience for the twins. "We were taken away from the people that really loved us and took care of us. It was a completely different world when we moved to Virginia," Ann recalled.

Ann's father spent about eighteen years in military service and then moved from one job to another until he was hired as a computer manager for a government agency. He had a "drinking problem." It was the reason for the breakdown of the marriage. Ann said she never saw her father drunk until about a year after she and her sister went to live with him in Virginia. She believes he began to use liquor again because of continuing tension in the marriage and because of the incest that was now becoming a part of Ann and Tammy's life after the mother's remarriage.

There were indications that Ann's father was a volatile man.

She recalled that on one occasion he had hit her so hard that she fell through a door. She also remembers that her father held her mother over his knees and paddled her. "That was just about the worst thing in the world," she said. "And if Mamma was sick, Daddy would run around the house throwing a temper tantrum. Mamma would say that it was his way of showing that he cared."

Ann hated her father, yet she also felt that her mother treated her father unfairly. "We felt sorry for Daddy and how he was being abused by Mamma. She could get anything she wanted from him if she hurt him bad enough. And so when Mamma would talk to us about Daddy and tell us what a bastard he was, we would say: 'Mamma, you don't give Daddy much chance. You constantly take from him and yet nothing he does is ever good enough.' I guess we just thought Mamma was not fair to Daddy and we had to sort of protect him," Ann concluded.

The incestuous relation between Ann and her father also involved her sister, Tammy. The incestuous behavior always took place simultaneously when both were forced to engage in sexual relations with their father. Ann recalled how the incest began. "We were in the fifth grade. Our teacher sent a note home saying the movies about menstruation would be shown to the class and asked the parents to give their consent. Mother read the note and talked to Daddy about it. When we came home from school the next day, Daddy was home from work. We both sensed that something was not right," Ann recalled. "Daddy told us he thought the movie was a fine idea, but that he and mother thought we ought to know more about sex. He asked us to go with him into the bathroom. And then he stripped down and said we had to learn about male anatomy, how and why it operated like it did. At first it was just touching. We would touch him and then he would touch us, our breasts and other parts of our bodies. He always did this with both of us at the same time. I think it was because he knew that if it just happened to one of us, we would have gone to somebody and told them about it."

Ann's father cautioned the twins not to ever reveal to their mother what was happening because it would "really kill her," so the sexual relationship continued unabated until the day that a quarrel broke out between Ann and her mother. "I remember that we had brought home our report cards from school and I had gotten an F in one of my subjects. When mother came home from work and saw my report card, she laid into both me and Tammy. She said we were both stupid and no good and that she should never have had us." Ann remembered that Daddy had told her mother, "You should have put them in an orphanage and maybe they would have made something of themselves."

"I was washing dishes. Tammy was upstairs doing her household chores. We did almost all the housework for Mamma. I was really upset. I told Mamma I wanted to talk to her and she tried to walk away. I remember that I grabbed her by the shoulder and told her she had better listen to what I had to say. That I got an F because I had to do all the housework and didn't have time to do my homework. And then I told her about what was going on between Daddy and my sister and me."

Ann's mother confronted her husband with what Ann had told her. Ann said she could overhear the conversation. "Daddy said to mother that she ought to know what little bitches those children are; their grandmother trained them to be whores." He denied that there was any sexual relation between himself and the daughters. Ann's mother accepted his denial. She told Ann's father, "I knew Ann was lying to me. I know you never did anything wrong. It's just those children's wild daydreams." Then her mother cried because she thought her children hated her and were out to hurt her.

Because Ann's mother did not protect her, the incest continued. In fact, Ann believed that her mother actually encouraged the father's continuing to sexually harass her and Tammy. "There were times when Mamma would encourage Daddy to drink in the evenings before bedtime," Ann recalled. "She would tell him she liked him better if he was drinking. Then she would go off to bed and Daddy would come after me and Tammy. Daddy used Coke® bottles to put inside us. And he would put clothes pins on our nipples. I had very long hair and Daddy would take my hair and wrap it around Tammy's legs."

As Tammy and Ann began to sexually mature, their father became jealous of any association they had with boys. He frequently questioned them about having sex with the boys at school. "He would even check our sanitary napkins," Ann said, "to see if we were lying to him. I remember that one time we went out with some of our classmates to get leaves for our botany collection. When we came home that afternoon he sent us upstairs and he checked us out to make sure we had not been having sex." The father was also overly protective and on one occasion requested that the girls' Sunday school teacher chaperone them at a Valentine's Day dance, and he insisted on accompanying them to and from the school even though it was only across the street from where the family lived.

Ann and her sister had few friends and they seldom associated with other poeple. "My sister and I thought we were wearing a scarlet letter, that people knew what we were. We didn't talk to people, even the kids at school. We just stayed away. The only conservation we had was with each other. I guess we felt that we were being punished," Ann continued. "We were punished because we weren't really wanted, because we shouldn't have been born."

At one point, Ann sought the help of her school counselor and decided to confide in her. After she had told the counselor what was happening, the counselor told Ann that she wished she had not given her this information and that they had just better pretend that it had not taken place and "that you never told me any of this." Ann had considered suicide as a way of out of her incestuous relations, "but I couldn't do that because it would have hurt my grandmother and grandfather. They always told us life was good and precious and that we should enjoy it to the fullest," said Ann. She had also considered the possibility of going to "someone who would operate on me so I couldn't get pregnant. I was under the impression from what I had heard from some girls at school that maybe I could go to someone and have everything cut out, then I wouldn't even get pregnant and Daddy could do anything he wanted and nobody would find out. There wouldn't have been any obvious sign of what was going on if I didn't get pregnant."

But at age thirteen, Ann was pregnant as a result of her father's continuing sexual exploitation. She had a miscarriage and was hospitalized when she ran a high temperature from the infection caused by a lack of medical attention. At the hospital, the attending physician seemed willing to listen to what Ann wanted to tell him about the incestuous relationship that caused the miscarriage. Ann's mother became suspicious, feared that the doctor would investigate the case and asked that he withdraw from treating Ann. Another doctor was called to attend Ann. He put a diagnosis of appendicitis in the medical record and performed an appendectomy.

How Incest Begins

Ann's experience reveals how incest relationships develop between fathers and daughters. Most fathers do not intentionally set out to seduce their daughters. The incestuous relationship develops gradually because the father is attempting to find a source of personal fulfillment that is lacking in his life and because he stands in need of recovering his self-esteem. He turns to the daughter who makes him feel loved and gives him a sense of competence and pride; he is trying to solve the problems of male menopause which is an emotionally stressful period. Many men cope with the male menopause problem by becoming involved in an extramarital relationship with a younger woman to restore their image of a vital youthful person. Incestuous fathers, however, do not want to become involved in an extramarital relationship. Instead, they look to their daughters to fill their sexual needs when their sexual fantasies are not satisfied by their wives.

Ann's father became involved in incest in his late forties — a period when the male begins to have doubts about his sexual virility and needs reassurance that he is attractive to women. He not only faced sexual rejection from his wife and began to wonder about his sexual potency during this time in his life but he was not certain that as a person he was of much worth to his family. It is also clear that the father was subjected to criticism and verbal attacks from her because of his personal inadequacies. Ann and her sister both regarded these attacks on their father as unfair and came to his defense. In turn, their father used the incestuous relationship to bolster his ego and restore his self-esteem. Incestuous fathers often exploit their daughters' admiration to fortify their sense of power and adequacy. The young child sees in the father a strong and adequate person, someone who deserves respect and affection. When the daughter responds to his sexual advances, the father achieves a sense of sexual adequacy and competence that his wife does not afford.

Closely related to the father's low self-esteem is his need to gain power and a sense of mastery over his daughter. Having seduced her and having gained access to her sexually not only restores his sense of competence but it also satisfies his need to dominate women. Some clinicians have discovered that incest may involve strong feelings of anger that can be traced back to the father's early childhood because of maternal rejection or domination. When these hostile feelings have not been adequately resolved, they may be acted out through sexual assaults or mild forms of sadism against women. In Ann's case, the father's behavior included some forms of sadistic sexual acts: pinching the girls' nipples with clothespins, inserting objects into their vaginas and using their hair to inflict pain. Inflicting pain and humiliation were integrated into the incestuous activity. The father's verbal abuse of Ann and her sister were further indications of his hostility and his need to demean females. Accounts of incest victims are often filled with descriptions of perverse and painful sexual activity, extensive use of obscene language and various forms of personal humiliation by incestuous fathers. In such cases, the father may be unconsciously working out his hostility toward his mother, wife or other female figure through engaging in sadistic sexual activity with his daughter.

The seduction of the daughter may also satisfy the father's desire to compensate for his wife's sexual rejection. If he cannot have free access to his wife, he will take his daughter as payment for the wife's failure to meet his sexual demands. Ann's father used his wife's coldness as a reason to turn to her and her sister for gratification of his sexual needs. Some researchers believe that men who turn to daughters in these cases are essentially passive and are so insecure that they do not want to risk failure in trying to seduce an adult woman. Their daughters present a convenient and nonthreatening opportunity for sexual gratification and are therefore preferred to adult sexual partners outside the family circle. Some men also view an incestuous relationship as "less sinful" than an extramarital relationship. In other cases, the incestuous relationship is part of a pattern of sexual promiscuity; all women are regarded as suitable sex objects, and daughters are considered to be legitimate sources of sexual gratification.

Some incestuous fathers compartmentalize their lives, somehow separating their sexual relationship with their daughters from all other aspects of their behavior. The Justices cite a case in which the incestuous father was a highly religious man. He and his wife were both active in church affairs. The children were baptized and taught to say prayers at home; the family always said prayers before meals. The parents had serious discussions with the daughter about sexual behavior and about morals. Yet, her father attempted sexual intercourse with her when she was eight years old, and the incestuous relationship continued until she was sixteen. The daughter recalled under hypnosis that her father played "the love game" with her as often as five times per week. Commenting on this behavior, the Justices observe that his behavior demonstrates that fathers maintain a dual image while they are involved in incest. "He worked, he had friends, he went to church, he committed incest . . . What dad did with the daughter was something completely apart and separate. A supreme rationalizer, he called it love."[1]

Incestuous fathers usually find some way of explaining and rationalizing their incestuous behavior. Ann's father said it was necessary for him to teach his daughters about sex. Research indicates that this is one of the most common rationalizations used to justify incestuous relationships that begin under the guise of sex education. Doctor Richard Sarles cites the case of a stepfather who told his stepdaughter that he wanted to initiate her into sex "so she could learn to do it right and not get hurt." He noted that this type of father is often surprised when other persons disapprove of this type of sex education. Some of them state, as did Ann's father, that it is their duty to teach their daughters the facts of life. Doctor Karpman described a case in which the father began to instruct his fifteen-year-old daughter about sex by exhibiting his penis and asking her to stroke it. The daughter explained how her father educated her further after she had been taught to masturbate him. "Dad assumed the teacher role. This was to overcome the guilt of further intimacies in which we were to indulge.

He wanted to show me the position the man assumes in sex relations. He had me spread my legs far apart until he was touching me with his penis. I did as I was told, assuming the role of an obedient child."[2]

Some fathers tell their daughters that they are doing them a service by providing sexual release and thereby preserving their virginity. They justify the sexual relationship with their daughters on the grounds that "she is going to get it somewhere and it is better to get it from me than from someone else." Doctor Rosenfeld points out that some fathers regard their daughters as their private property and argue that what they do in the privacy of the home does not concern other people. He cites the case of a father who asked his daughter to masturbate him daily from the time she was two years old. When authorities asked the father about this, he stated that it was a father's inherent right and natural prerogative to request sexual favors from his daughter.

However, most fathers begin to feel guilty or frightened after the sexual involvement becomes established. The father then begins to coerce his daughter into silence by warning her that if she discloses the secret relationship, the family will fall apart, she will bring disgrace on herself, and that she will probably be separated from the family and sent to a correctional institution. During this time, the father has a strong compulsion to repeat the incestuous experience and often induces the daughter into more extended and unusual forms of sexual behavior. The daughter usually tries to terminate the relationship as the father makes more sexual demands and as she becomes aware that other persons, particularly her mother, might discover what is happening. Most daughters also become resentful because their fathers use them as sexual objects by showing some affection during the sexual relationship, but more often refer to them as "bitch," "slut" or "whore."

Eventually, the daughter tries to escape from the incestuous relationship. She may turn to her mother, tell her what is happening and ask for her protection from further sexual abuse by the father. The response of the victim's mother varies. Some mothers accuse the daughter of fabricating the story or condemn her for having seduced the father. Other mothers accept the victim's story but refuse to take action that will terminate the relationship. One victim recalls that her mother reacted by saying, "They'll send your father to jail and we will all end up on welfare. Is that what you want to do to us?" It is no surprise that many incest victims come to feel responsible for the development of the incestuous relationship and sometimes bear the burden of blame for disclosing the secret relationship with their fathers.

The Father's Personality

Although much has been written about the causes of father-daughter incest, psychiatrists take different views as to the nature and extent of the psychiatric impairment that characterizes incestuous behavior. The incestuous father has been described as an immature, passive and timid person with low self-esteem and a fear of adult women. Others have described such men as suffering from a compulsive disorder, while some see incest as a situational disorder found in immature men who engage in incest when they are intoxicated. Some psychiatrists stress the view that sex with the daughter is based on the father's attempt to recover the maternal love that he needs to help him function as an adult.

One type of personality that has been identified as associated with many incestuous fathers is the sociopathic personality. These fathers are essentially asocial individuals who are driven by uncontrolled drives, are unable or unwilling to delay gratification of their wishes and tend to be highly aggressive. Most of the fathers in this group of offenders deny any sense of guilt and seem unconcerned about the damage that their behavior has inflicted on their daughters. The following case is an example of how these individuals view their incestuous relationships with their daughters.

A twenty-eight-year-old man admitted to sexually abusing his eight-year-old daughter from the age of eighteen months on. He denied having sexual intercourse with her and when faced with medical evidence said, "She must have been screwing around with someone else." He also stated that his daughter had voluntarily complied with his sexual advances, although the daughter had actually protested against his sexual advances when she was four years old. The father blamed the wife for what happend because she did not have intercourse with him often enough and left him

alone with the children. The father had his first sexual experience
with a fourteen-year-old sister when he was five years old. When
he was eleven, he had oral sex with a six-year-old female cousin.
He stated quite candidly that he thought of people as "things
placed here for my use and enjoyment." When questioned about
the incestuous relation to the daughter he dismissed it by saying,
"That's an old issue."[3]

Some cases of father-daughter incest fit into a concept that
Doctor Lloyd Wells had described as *restricted psychopathy*.
These fathers' behaviors are similar to that of the sociopath, but
these asocial traits are limited to restricted areas. The psychopathology is "sealed off in one corner" and does not permeate the
individual's entire character and behavior. In these cases, the
father's sociopathic personality is apparent in relationship to the
daughter and is restricted to the incestuous relationship. Inability
to postpone gratification, impulsiveness and absence of any feelings of guilt are evident in the incest relationship but not in other
areas of his life. Doctor Wells cites the case of a father who ex-
hibited the traits of restricted psychopathy. The father openly
admitted that he had been involved sexually with his thirteen-year-
old daughter for the past two years. He claimed to have had a fixation about pubescent girls, having had intercourse with a ten-
year-old sister when he was six years old and with a younger
sister throughout much of his childhood. He said that his sexual
involvement with his daughter was primarily a means of showing
affection, and that "I just wanted to be a good dad to her and
have her like me." His wife described the father as a considerate,
kind and affectionate person, saying that he was a good provider
and a prominent member of the community. The father was embarrassed because several members of the church had found out
about the incest. During the course of exploring the problem, the
father and mother began to place major responsibility on the
daughter and then seemed to reestablish a satisfactory marital
relationship even though the mother had originally threatened to
divorce her husband. This pattern of incest is characteristic of the
restricted psychopath, who is a rather well-adjusted member of
the community but turns to a daughter for sexual gratification
through a process of rationalization that makes his conduct ac-

ceptable to himself.

Society tends to see men who have incestuous relationships with their daughters as social outcasts, severely alcoholic, psychotic or mentally retarded. Some incestuous fathers are indeed alcoholic or psychotic. Some do have undesirable personality traits such as lack of self-control and lack of an ordered way of living, but the majority of incest offenders do not have severe mental disorders. Maisch found only one father who was truly mentally ill among sixty-seven offenders who came to the attention of the courts. Approximately 50 percent were psychologically normal persons.[4] Most incestuous fathers appear to be unexceptional. They look after their families reasonably well and are not radically different from other men.

During the early thirties, the view that incestuous fathers were men with unusually strong sex drives or sex degenerates was put forward to explain incestuous behavior. However, more recent research indicates that this view is not supported by scientific evidence. The Kinsey Institute studies on sexual behavior indicated that men who commit incest have a low frequency of sexual urges compared to other types of sex offenders. Maisch also found that incestuous fathers did not have excessive desires for sexual intercourse compared to other married men. The view that the father turns to the daughter for sexual gratification because of his excessive need for sexual intercourse appears to be contrary to what is known about the sexual life of incest offenders.

There is evidence to support the view that alcoholism is a prominent characteristic feature of many incest situations. Maisch found that one-fifth to one-fourth of the offenders had serious problems with alcohol and concluded that the loss of self-control due to excessive use of alcohol was a significant predisposing factor in 21 percent of the cases that came to the attention of the court.[5] Gebhard comes to a similar conclusion regarding the use of alcohol as a factor related to incestous behavior.[6] Over one-third of the incest victims in Herman's survey considered their fathers to be problem drinkers, but the drinking was carefully concealed from those outside the family.[7] Neither the father nor the family recognized the drinking as a serious medical problem because the father was able to carry on satisfactorily at work and his social behavior was acceptable. A thirty-two-year-old woman who was sexually abused by her father recalled that he never admitted that he used alcohol, although empty bottles belied his denial. Despite his use of alcohol, the father was able to carry on a successful medical practice. The daughter stated: "Everyone thought he was a wonderful person and a really fine doctor. I used to listen to other people tell me what a great doctor he was and how well he treated his patients. I would think to myself, what if they really knew what was going on at home?" In this case, as in many others, the father did not seek medical or psychiatric treatment for his alcoholism.

When alcohol is involved in the incestuous behavior, most victims recall that the sexual advances were made when the father had been drinking. Some are inclined to attribute their father's incestuous behavior to the influence of alcohol, and in some cases, the offender uses the drinking as an excuse for making sexual advances on his daughter. More often than not, the sexual assault was planned in advance, and on careful questioning, offenders often admit that they drink in order to gather the courage to approach their daughters sexually.

One of the predominant personality traits of incestuous fathers is their authoritarian, sometimes tyrannical and absolute rule over the family. Many incestuous fathers brook no opposition on any account and rely on intimidation to control other family members. Some use force or actual beatings to gain submission to their wishes, while outside the family they present themselves as sympathetic and admirable men. One incest victim described how her father dominated the family by the use of force and violence:

> It was definitely my father who was head of the home. I began to realize that other fathers were not like that. I may have done some things that deserved punishment, but you don't have to beat someone until their back is red and bleeding. He was especially abusive to my younger brother. I remember one time he had taken in some little kittens. And my father destroyed them by throwing rocks on the kittens' heads until they were dead.

A survey conducted by Blair and Rita Justice indicated that

approximately 20 percent of incestuous fathers included in the study could be classified as "tyrants." Some of these tyrants had a tendency to drink, but they were not actually addicted to alcohol. "Many tyrants disguise their need for closeness through macho attitudes toward sex," write Blair and Rita Justice. "They believe that one mark of being a real man is to be sexually active and powerful, so for them sex is not for closeness but for expressing manly virility."[8]

Jealousy often develops on the part of fathers who regard the daughter as belonging to them exclusively. They are highly suspicious of any other males who threaten to break the sexual relationship with their daughters. They become enraged if they see their daughters speaking to a boy their own age. They exercise complete control over the daughter's life, including relationships outside the family as illustrated in this case where the jealousy of the father was carried to the extreme.

> A forty-five-year-old man worked as a civil servant and was regarded as irreproachable at work. The marriage and the family life had suffered from the outset because of the father's personality. He would beat his wife on the least pretext. He ruled despotically over all the members of the family and would not tolerate opposition. Even before it came to incest he controlled his daughter's every word and action, tried to isolate her socially, examined her clothes for signs of sperm and became paranoidically jealous.

While there is no one type of incestuous father, most men who become involved in incest with their daughters share a common problem: they long for a sense of intimacy and hunger for closeness and warmth, usually because they did not experience adequate nurturing and felt deprived during their childhood. As adults, they reach out for gratification of the basic need to be loved, and they turn to their daughters in the hope that here they will find a source of love. The difficulty confronting these fathers lies in their inability to distinguish between sex and affection. For them, affection can be expressed only in a physical, sexual relationship. As Blair and Rita Justice point out, "He does not know how to be close and affectionate in a nonsexual sense or how to meet his needs to belong and have a warm relationship

but affection doesn't seem to be the point, gratification does

affection expressed
vs.
affection sought

in a nonphysical way. He turns to sex with his own daughter in an attempt to meet these needs. He is seldom aware of what he is needing from the daughter. Most men who commit incest are completely out of touch with their needs and have no experience in meeting them in healthy ways."[9]

The Mother's Personality

The mother's role in developing and maintaining a sexual relationship between her husband and her daughter has been examined by several researchers. Some psychiatrists argue that the mother provides the key to the incestuous relationship and that she is at least unconsciously sanctioning the incest. They point out that the mothers in these families often have strong dependency needs and that many have experienced physical or psychological desertion during their childhood. As a consequence, they have difficulty in functioning as independent adults and have more than ordinary problems in assuming the role of wife and mother. Having received little affection and nurturing from their own mothers, they cast their daughters into the maternal role. The daughters of these mothers often report that they began to take over major responsibilities such as keeping house, caring for their younger siblings and preparing meals for the family. Eventually, this role reversal of mother and daughter may place the daughter in a position where she is called upon to meet the sexual needs of the father.

Some research supports the view that the mother's incapacity is physical, rather than psychological, and that the role reversal is a result of her health problems. David Finkelhor found that girls whose mothers were often ill were almost twice as likely to be sexually abused in childhood compared to average girls. The study indicated that 35 percent of the women whose mothers were chronically ill had been sexually abused as children. Maisch reported that 33 percent of the mothers in incestuous families suffered from a serious physical illness.[10] Herman found that half of the daughters remembered that their mothers had periods of disabling illnesses that resulted in frequent hospitalizations. One-third of them had been separated from their mothers for an extended period because their mothers' illness made it

"Tyrants" (20%) a significantly higher percentage than the

impossible for them to care for their children. Depression, alcoholism and psychosis were among the most common causes of the mother's disability. Many daughters commented about the strange nature of the maladies that seemed to afflict their mothers. For the most part, the mother's psychiatric and medical problems went undiagnosed and untreated.[11] role depression →oppression

Customarily, the mother assumes the duties of caring for the husband and the children in our society. If the mother is unable to carry out the nurturing role, it usually falls upon the daughter. The oldest daugher is most often the family member who takes over the mother's role when she becomes incapacitated. Herman points out that the father does not take over the mother's usual tasks but assumes that it is his right to continue to receive the services formerly provided by his wife from his daughter, including sexual services. "This view of the father's prerogative to be served not only is shared by the fathers and daughters in these families, but is often encouraged by social attitudes. Fathers who feel abandoned by their wives are not generally expected or taught to assume primary parenting responsibilities. We should not find it surprising, then, the fathers occasionally turn to their daughters for services (domestic and sexual) that they had formerly expected from their wives."[12]

Studies of incest uniformly point out that there is an underlying alienation in mother-daughter relationships in incestuous families. Many daughters saw their mothers as inherently weak and powerless. Others remembered their mothers with feelings of contempt and hostility, pictured them as uncaring and rejecting persons who afforded little gratification for their emotional needs. They sometimes described their mothers as cruel and unfeeling, as reflected in the following statements of incest victims:

I really don't like my mom. I guess I am bitter. She's very selfish. She was seventeen when she had me, and her mother put her in a home. She blames me for ruining her life because she got pregnant with me. But I'm not the one who spread my legs.

Why do people bother having kids? Why did my mother have me? I'm sure in those days people knew how to get rid of them. She seemed to know how. I wish she was dead so I could forget about her — or that I was dead so that she'd suffer. Why does God allow people like her to live?

For many daughters, the mother presents something of an enigma. Katherine Brady recalls that she often hoped that her mother would try to talk to her father when he was especially irritable and inquire into the reasons for his black moods. "Sooner or later, I felt, she would have to ask him what was behind his moods, and I wanted her to . . . I wanted the whole thing to blow up, blow wide open. I wanted to get rid of my terrible secret." At times, her mother would threaten to leave and take the children with her, but when Katherine's father behaved more pleasantly, she dropped the matter and did not try to get at the cause of the problem. Katherine Brady came to the conclusion that her mother had really abandoned her.

> When dad made a brief effort to behave more pleasantly, she inquired no further. This said two things to me: that she didn't really want to know what was troubling him — she demanded that he change his behavior but didn't ask what was causing it — and that she had power, but wouldn't or couldn't use it in my behalf. I resented her terribly for both these things. I could sometimes make excuses for dad: initial good motive, an abnormal sex drive, loving feelings for me, estrangement from mother. But for mother there were none. She had abandoned me again.[13]

Some daughters pictured their mothers as weak and powerless, women who felt defenseless against their husbands and submitted to them because the marriage had to be preserved at all costs. These daughters described their mothers as martyrs who endured suffering and hardship as part of their lot as wives and mothers. One said of her mother: "She was nothing but a floor mat. She sold herself out and her self-respect. She was a love slave to my father." Clinical reports tend to confirm that many mothers in incestuous families are essentially passive and dependent women who lack the independence and self-sufficiency to interfere in the incestuous relationship. Because they view the husband as the only source of security, such dependent women feel totally helpless to control their own lives. They not only experience feelings of powerlessness but they also derive no sense of personal fulfillment within the family. Therefore, they often endure hardship without taking steps to change their lives or find a solution to the problems within the family. As Yvonne Tormes observes, the husband can easily undermine the already weak ego of the mother and pursue his incestuous relationship with the daughter without fear of interference. "By brutality and superior initiative, her husband has nullified her roles as mother and wife. Even prior to tolerating the incest, she seems to have tolerated an increasing amount of deviant behavior, violent and nonviolent, from him and her forebearance seems to have encouraged his progress to the incest offense."

The incestuous daughter pays the price for the mother's sense of powerlessness and her submission to the father. Because the mother feels that she cannot survive without her husband's economic and emotional support, the daughter is extremely vulnerable to the father's sexual demands. As Herman points out: "Rather than provoke her husband's anger or risk his desertion, she will capitulate. If the price of marriage includes the sexual sacrifice of her daughter, she will raise no objections. Her first loyalty is to her husband, regardless of his behavior. She sees no other choice."[14]

Lack of sexual response or outright rejection by the wife is frequently cited as a significant factor in setting the stage for an incestuous father-daughter relationship. Miasch reports that 52 percent of the offenders said that they had unsatisfactory sexual relationships with their wives, and they described their sexual partners as frigid, cold or not interested in sex. The mothers in this sample rejected sexual relations outright or made excuses for withdrawing from sexual intercourse with their husbands. The Justices point out that in many cases the problem begins when the sex stops between father and mother. "The most common overt event preceding the onset of incest between father and daughter is sexual estrangement between the mother and father," they write. "This estrangement most often takes place as a result of increasing tension and hostility between father and mother, but it may also come as a result of the mother's entering a hospital, going to work at night, taking a trip."[15] The personal accounts of incest victims often refer to the father's deprivation of sexual gratification as the reason for the development of the incestuous relationship. In some instances, the daughter is inclined to accept the mother's sexual rejection of her father as being in fact true. But in other cases, the daughter doubts the father's statement or wonders why he does not seek sexual gratification outside the family if his needs are not being met by her mother. "I can't comprehend why he would come to a twelve-year-old girl," one victim stated. "I would much rather he had gone outside the marriage and to another woman to fill his needs."

Lack of sexual gratification may indeed be a precipitating factor in the development of incest, but it is usually only one of a number of conditions that lead to an incestuous experience. Many couples face some difficulty in their sexual relationship during the course of their marriage, but the husband does not turn to his daughter as a substitute for his wife. Moreover, the sexual estrangement is not necessarily an indication that the wife is frigid. Sexual dissatisfaction and complaints of frigidity are often evidence of a more general emotional disturbance in the relationship between the parents; the sexual alienation is symptomatic of a serious difficulty in the marrriage and is not an indication of sexual dysfunctioning on the part of the wife. In the final analysis, the sexual availability of the mother is not the principal problem in the eventual development of an incestuous relationship. The sexual problem is a reflection that the emotional life of the family is seriously deficient in some important respects. The parents both experience deprivation in some segment of their lives, a lack of nurturing, of affection and concern. The incest is generated out of this deprivation; the sexual problems of the parents reflect this lack of fulfillment, and within this context the incestuous relationship has its origin.

Perhaps the one personality trait that is shared by all mothers of incestuous families is very low self-esteem. They think of themselves as unimportant, place little value on themselves as persons and are plagued by a sense of doubt about their adequacy. Daughters become aware of the mother's low self-esteem, see her play a submissive role in the family and come to the conclusion that women are indeed powerless, and that the best way to survive is to follow their mother's example. It is not surprising, therefore, that when their fathers begin to make sexual demands, these daughters become easy prey for sexual exploitation and abuse. The following case illustrates how an incestuous relationship develops when mothers feel powerless, dependent and insecure.

Carol is the mother of six children: one daughter age sixteen and five sons ranging in age from fourteen to twenty-four. Her daughter was involved in an incestuous relation with her father for almost ten years. The mother was not aware of the sexual abuse until her daughter was age thirteen. Looking back on the experience, Carol feels that as the mother she has some responsibility for what happened to her daughter. She is convinced that her low self-esteem was one of the key factors that maintained the incestuous relationship over a period of ten years. "It is easy to see why my daughter was victimized for so many years, feeling as she did and, yes, how I had taught her to feel by my role model," says Carol. "She felt that she couldn't tell anyone because who would believe her anyway? After all, men are always right and women never are right about anything."

Carol married at a very young age and was dependent on her husband from the very outset. As she put it: "I went from my parents telling me what to do, to my husband telling me. I never questioned this." She felt that her own needs were unimportant and the needs of her husband came first. Her husband reinforced Carol's feeling of worthlessness; he was emotionally abusive and dominated the entire family. He was a heavy drinker, and when he was drinking there was always the threat of violence. Carol recalled that she underwent long periods of depression, times when she felt "terrible about myself." She explained how her husband dominated her life: "He really knew how to keep me down. He made me feel worthless as a woman. It still hurts sometimes when I think of how I really bought into all the things he kept telling me. In the frame of mind I was in, it is no wonder that I was so unaware of what was happening. I believed women weren't important anyway."

Because Carol felt so inadequate and worthless, she also permitted her husband to dominate the daughter's life. The pattern continued unabated, making it possible for the father to exploit the mother's lack of self-confidence and passivity. The daughter felt that her mother could not really protect her from the father's sexual demands. Moreover, the mother's passivity led the daughter to believe that if she told anyone about what was happening the family would fall apart. "For all those years my daugher endured the pain because she didn't think I could make it on my own," Carol explained. "She was afraid the family would break apart and that someone or everyone would blame her. She also felt that I would be so hurt and so would everybody else in the family if she told. She rationalized it this way: As long as she kept the secret, no one was being hurt but her."

Carol is now a staff member of a rape information service where she counsels victims of incest and their families. She believes that children are often victims of their mother's low self-esteem. She writes:

> Never in my experience have I seen a mother whose children are victimized within the family feel confident and sure of herself. Therefore a woman who is submissive and has a low self-image is a very poor role model and sets the stage for incest to occur. This is why we so often hear of the mother who was aware of the abuse and did nothing to stop it or help her child. She is so unsure of her own capabilities, so overwhelmed by her husband. She has submitted so much of herself, her wants and needs, her very being. She bows once again to his power over her.[16]

Carol's experience supports the view that if the mother is non-assertive and defers to her husband continually, the daughter perceives women as weak, mindless and incapable. Incest victims usually do not find a model of a strong and autonomous mother to follow as they are growing up in an incestuous family. They have no example of someone who can say "no" to the father. It is not surprising then that they take on their mother's life-style, submit to being dominated by their father and finally give in to his demands for sexual gratification.

The Daughter's Personality

Researchers and clinicians have examined the psychological traits and personal characteristics of incest victims to determine how and why certain daughters become involved in an incestuous relationship with their fathers. Studies indicate that many of the victims have deep and serious feelings of personal failure and inadequacy. They often see themselves as unattractive and unlovable. Herman's study of a group of 40 incest victims indicated that 60 percent of the women had a predominately negative self-image and that 32 percent had a confused self-image. Maisch found that victims showed symptoms of depression in 28 percent of the cases studied. The depressive symptoms were manifested in feelings of being oppressed or being in a condition of complete helplessness and hopelessness. Six of the girl victims had attempted suicide and two others had thoughts of suicide.[17] Herman also found suicide attempts were made by 37 percent of the women who had been involved in incest.[18] The depression and suicidal tendencies either accompanied the incest or were a result of the guilt and shame connected with the incestuous behavior. But, in many cases, the feelings of personal inadequacy and unattractiveness were present before the incest began, indicating that the victim may sometimes find compensation for negative feelings through the attention she gains from the father when she grants him sexual gratification.

In short, the incest brings some rewards — both in a material and psychological sense. Fathers usually do not use force to induce their daughters into a sexual relationship. Instead, they seduce the victim by flattery, expressions of affection and material rewards. Most victims recall that their fathers told them how much they loved them and how important their role was in providing happiness and sense of sexual fulfillment. Fathers also frequently give more than ordinary approval to the daughter, in contrast to their continual demeaning of their wives. In the early phases of the relationship, the daughter may find the father's displays of affection and his expressions of admiration a welcome source of emotional support, especially if her mother is indifferent or uncaring. She submits to the sexual advances because she feels in need of the father's approval and wants to please him in order to feel loved and wanted.

The power that the daughter gains through the sexual relationship with her father is also a source of gratification. She has a special position in the family because her father supports her in what she wants and will even make it possible for the daughter to tyr-

annize siblings who may stand in her way. She may also use the
sexual relationship to win matieral rewards and special privileges,
learning how to manipulate her father as part of the incestuous
bargaining process. Fathers make promises to their daughters in order to keep them from disclosing the secret relationship or give
them expensive gifts in exchange for sexual favors.

In many cases, the daughter actively seeks her father's approval because she wants to feel that she is attractive and that she is
capable of finding a man who will love her. The basic process of
rivalry between mother and daughter for the approval and affection of the father has been described in detail by Freud and his
successors. In nonincestuous families, the father does not attempt
to use the daughter to fulfill his own sexual needs, and the mother
is strong enough to prevent the father from having access to the
daughter. Herman made an interesting study in which she compared the relationship between seductive fathers and their families
to the fathers who were incestuous.[19] The seductive fathers dis-
played some sexual interest in their daughters but never attempted
to engage them in sexual contacts. The daughters whose fathers
were seductive but not incestuous also had a special position
in the family. They were often known as "daddy's princess"
or "daddy's special girl." In some important respects, the daughters of seductive fathers had some of the same problems as did
those who became involved in overt incest. Their fathers interfered
with their strivings for independence and autonomy, and, although the daughters appreciated their father's attention, they
resented his efforts to monopolize their time and control their
lives. Like the incest victims, many of these women also felt that
their mothers had sacrificed them to their fathers and had acqui-
esced in the relationship.

The daughters of seductive fathers were like the daughters
of incestuous fathers in some respects. They tended to hold
women in contempt and had a highly exaggerated sense of the importance of men. They also had problems in adult life that related
to feelings of inferiority to men. However, they did not develop
a sense of negative identity because they did not feel the shame
and guilt that were part of the life of the incest victims. "They did
not think of themselves as irredeemably evil and did not feel

doomed to exclusion from normal society," concluded Herman. "As a result, they were spared some of the worst punishment of the incest victim. They felt neither obliged to submit to physical abuse from others, nor to make attempts to destroy themselves." However, Herman observes that covert and overt incest are derived from a common source, namely, the tendency for women to undervalue themselves and to overvalue men.

The daughter's level of self-esteem is important in determining whether overt incest will occur, and the mother's level of self-esteem is equally important. If the mother is able to function adequately and does not submit to emotional and physical abuse by her husband, the daughter can be protected from an overt sexual relationship with her father even though he has a sexual interest in her. Herman believes:

> The families in which mothers were rendered unusually powerless, whether through battering, physical disability, mental illness or the burden of repeated childbearing, appeared to be particularly at risk for the development of overt incest. In families where a more nearly equal balance of parental power was preserved, overt incest did not develop, even though the fathers' sexual interest in their daughters was quite apparent.[20]

The father's sexual interest in the daughter is usually heightened when she reaches puberty, making adolescence a particulaly critical period in the life of the maturing daughter. During this period, the daughter must learn to deal with the problems of her sexual and personal identity. Her sexual drives are beginning to emerge and break into full awareness. During this time of physiological and psychological change the father begins to have sexual feelings toward her. Maisch observed that sexual approaches by the father or stepfather are frequently motivated by such physical changes as the development of breasts and rounding of the buttocks when the daughter reaches puberty. In 73 percent of the cases, the daughter had reached menarche when the first episode of incest took place. Maisch concluded that the beginning of sexual attractiveness associated with adolecent daughters is an important factor in incest: "It is certainly the case that the age of the victim, more precisely the biological age of the daughter, is, as a rule, of great significance for the father or stepfather. The development of the female body has a stimulating effect for many men and may trigger incestuous behavior." Maisch cites the case of a forty-three-year-old man who carried on an incestuous relationship with his daughter for two years. He told authorities that when his daughter reached fourteen she had just had her first period. "She was already quite a young woman," he said, "and the shape of her body excited me." He made various pretexts to get his wife to change their normal sleeping arrangment so that the daughter could share the bed with her father. About six months after this change in sleeping arrangements took place, the daughter was introduced to sexual relationships by her father.

Some fathers see their daughters as actually initiating the sexual relationship through their provocative sexual behavior and view them as sexually precocious girls who are sexually curious and voluntarily enter into the incestuous experience. This view of the incest victim as another Lolita who takes great satisfaction in seducing her father with her sexual charms and winning smile is shared by many people who hold the daughter responsible for enticing the father to commit incest. However, evidence to support this view is not found in the scientific literature. In fact, scientific studies indicate that only a very small percentage of victims take the initiative in forming an incestuous relationship. Maisch reported that only two out of seventy-six girls included in the study actually provoked the fathers to break the incest barrier. For the most part, the sexual behavior of the girls who were involved in incest did not differ from that of their contemporaries in this respect.[22]

Although the overwhelming majority of incest victims do not provoke sexual advances from their fathers, very few actively resist the first attempts of the father to involve them in sexual interaction. At the outset of the incest experience, most daughters are inclined to passively accept the father's advances and are even tolerant of his sexual behavior. The absence of strong resistance to the father's initiative is not surprising in view of the special nature of an incestuous relationship. A daughter or stepdaughter finds herself in a set of circumstances that is quite different than if she were being attacked by a total stranger, because the father is someone whom she thinks she can trust. Moreover, she is emotionally dependent on her father and she is hesitant to reject him for fear of losing his love and approval.

The incestuous experience evokes varied responses from the daughter. Some victims are surprised and bewildered by what is happening. They have mixed feelings of fear and sexual curiosity. Some are repulsed and disgusted by their father's sexual behavior and simulate sleep to avoid participating in the sexual activity. The experience may have pleasurable aspects, mixed with feelings of anger and shame. Katherine Brady explains:

> Since I had to, I might as well enjoy it. But the enjoyment was not unmixed. He sucked my breasts, and I felt wildly excited and terribly angry. He entered me with his finger, and I felt a surge of hate combined with desire. I tried as much as I could to mute my response. Still, he saw my excitement, and a grin spread across his face.[23]
>
> When he and I were having sex, I tried to deny myself orgasms, doing everthing possible to divorce myself from the sexual moment. I found ways to make myself absent — ways to go out of focus, to pretend it wasn't happening. And I also learned to pretend that it was, faking orgasms to bring episodes to an end.[24]

Daughters sometimes do blame themselves for becoming involved in sexual relations with their fathers. They begin to wonder what they might have done to bring about the incest and consider themselves to be sick, bad and evil persons. Often, these feelings of guilt and shame follow the victims into adult life long after the incestuous relationship has ended.

Some incest victims have a history of delinquent and antisocial behavior that began in childhood and preceded the incestuous relationship. These victims are found to have been badly neglected and mistreated as children. Deprived of a normal childhood and subjected to indifference and abuse by their parents, they developed severe personality disturbances. The following case illustrates how a nineteen-year-old girl became involved in an incestuous relationship for five years with her stepfather.

Joan was first entered on the police records when she was arrested for several episodes of stealing money. After she was arrested, she attempted to commit suicide with sleeping pills, and an investigation was undertaken to determine the cause of her depression. The investigation revealed that Joan was born out of wedlock. She was an unwanted child of a mother who had been hospitalized because of a mental illness. Her mother abused Joan and rejected her outright. Until she was eight years old, she was cared for mostly by her grandmother, and she never knew her father. Her mother remarried. Joan's stepfather was an unstable, weak and underachieving man, but he was the first person who ever adopted a friendly and caring attitude toward Joan at any time in her entire life. She soon came to regard her stepfather as a protector who shielded her from her harsh mother. It is no surprise that she responded to his demonstrations of affection and became involved in incest.

Studies indicate that girls who have been subjected to unhappy childhood experiences are especially susceptible to becoming involved in incest. Many victims have had an extremely unstable home life even before they reach the age of six. They have been shifted from one institution to another, from grandparents to foster parents, from a family with a father to a family with a stepfather. Because of these constantly changing life situations, many of these girls become confused about their roles. They lack the experience of a stable relationship wih a caring adult that is so important in the development of a normal childhood. The absence of a mother or a long period of separation from the mother before the age of six is particularly traumatic. Deprived of a normal childhood and having undergone frequent changes during their lives, these girls are responsive to the advances of a stepfather, as was Joan. Although deprivation and neglect do not invariably result in incest, children who undergo unhappy experiences early in their lives are more vulnerable than those who have received adequate nurturing from loving, caring parents.

Crisis and Stress

At one time or another, every family faces a crisis, a critical and emotionally hazardous event that may have a devastating effect on the family and the life of its members. When a crisis occurs, the life of the family is drastically changed in many impor-

tant respects, and these changes require fundamental social read-
justments in order to cope with the crisis. For example, the loss
of a parent through death, divorce or desertion places new and
additional responsibilities on the remaining parent who must see
to it that the family will survive. An extended period of unemployment can have serious consequences for the family. The loss
of income requires adjusting to a lower standard of living and a
different life-style. The father who prides himself on being the
breadwinner and "head of the household" may begin to feel that
he is not an adequate man because he is out of work. Or a mother's prolonged stay in a hospital for treatment of a serious illness
can disrupt the family's living pattern and create a host of difficulties because of her absence and her inability to carry out her
normal duties in caring for her children. Divorce often leaves one
or both partners feeling abandoned, lonely and isolated. Children
also feel the tension of marital conflict and have problems adjusting to their parents' separation.

Blair and Rita Justice conducted a study to determine the
extent to which change and stress could be identified in incestuous
families. They found that when they gave the Schedule of Recent
Experience or Social Readjustment Scale as a measure of stress
to 35 abusing parents and compared their scores to a matched
group of 35 nonabusing parents, the difference was highly significant. The abusing parents had an average score of 234 compared with 124 for the nonabusing group. Scores for incestuous
families averaged 240, indicating that these families had undergone
rapid and significant changes during the 12 months prior to the incest.[25] In one family, the father had undergone a change in occupation, residence, personal habits, finances and marriage. Although excessive change and the stress associated with change is
not in itself a cause of incest, it is a contributing factor, because it
brings out tendencies that might otherwise be kept under control.
"In some families, excessive change may go on for several years
before incest occurs, before a father lets go of the control he normally has over his behavior and turns to his daughter as a sexual
source of closeness and comfort," Blair and Rita Justice write.
"Although some changes are more critical than others in the incestuous family, all mount up in terms of collectively representing a

predisposing agent."[26] The case of Julia is an example of how excessive change and stress is an important predisposing agent.

Until Julia entered the sixth grade, her life was carefree and uneventful. Her father provided well for the family and her mother; although quite young, he was kind and affectionate to all six children. However, the father's occupation as a long-distance trucker kept him away from the family for weeks on end. Eventually his wife, lonely and isolated, struck up a relationship with a man who later became her lover. The mother's extramarital affair continued for several months, but her husband discovered that she had been unfaithful when he returned from a trip unexpectedly. Julia recalls that there was a "horrible fight, my mother screaming and blood all over her face where Daddy had beaten her." The next morning, Julia's mother left home and did not return. The divorce left Julia's father completely devastated. "He would just sit and drink for hours on end. And I had never seen him drunk before," Julia said. "I know that he must have loved my mother very much, and when she left us it was like the end of the world for him. I remember that he would cry a lot and he would want my sister and me to comfort him. I guess I was the one he turned to most. Everyone thought I was able to manage things better than my sister, and I think he thought of me as the one who was taking mother's place in his life. I know that one time when he was drinking and wanting to have sex, he even called me by my mother's name." Gradually, Julia did begin to take over what had been her mother's role in the family before the divorce. The father's drinking continued unabated. "He just seemed to drink and go to work," said Julia, "then he would come home and drink some more." Julia had some sympathy for her father, listened to him when he told her how miserable he was and how much she meant to him, especially now that her mother was no longer there to give him love and affection. Julia's concern and sympathy for her father gradually led to an intimate relation. "I think that when my father first began to be sexual with me I didn't really mind it. In fact, I really enjoyed it when he would caress me and even when he would put his hands under my dress and between my legs. My sister never did like it when my father began to do sexual things with my sister. But it wasn't like that to

affection turned to anger?

me . . . until he began to get real dirty and when he would want me to do things with my sister. But if I said I didn't want to do that, he would usually say 'okay' and he wouldn't make us do things we didn't want to do. Except the one time when he penetrated me. And that was how I lost my virginity. It really hurt, and after that my father didn't try to have intercourse with me again."

Julia's incestuous experiences with her father followed the discovery of his wife's affair, the episode of physical violence and the sudden departure of the mother. But less dramatic changes in the life of the family can produce tension and stress. An unsatisfactory marriage often leads to sexual problems that produce stress. Mother and father become emotionally and physically alienated and the father begins to feel the need for emotional and sexual gratification. When the marital and sexual life of the parents continues to bring little reward to either the husband or the wife, the father may turn to the daughter to reduce the stress he is undergoing. In some cases, the sexual estrangement between the parents results from a long-standing illness or absence of the mother for extended periods of time. Or the sexual problems may be brought on by the father's depression when he loses his job and suffers a loss of self-esteem. In either case, if the father cultivates a close relationship with the daughter to make up for the sexual deprivation, the possibility of incest is increased.

Julia's experience indicates that a combination of circumstances may lead to incest. Her father felt abandoned, lonely and isolated because of his wife's departure and the blow that her extramarital relation dealt to his ego. At the same time, Julia was developing into an attractive, sexually mature female. Her father was not oblivious to the physical changes that had taken place. "My father used to undress me and tell me how beautiful I was. He would fondle my breasts and tell me that I was going to get a lot of attention from boys because my body was beginning to fill out. Things like that did embarrass me, but I guess I liked it too because it made me feel like a woman, like I was someone really important." Like many other incest victims, Julia was flattered by the special attention she received from her father. Most daughters who feel deprived of other sources of emotional support appreci-

ate any sign of recognition and tenderness. When their fathers
shower them with special attention, praise and admiration, they
are especially susceptible to being led into an incestuous relationship. Julia also tried to act as a "rescuer" for her father. Sensing
that he was unhappy and needed someone to look after him, she
became the "lady of the house." When she took over the rescuer
role, she also satisifed her need to be important and gain her
father's approval.

Opportunity for Incest

Father-daughter incest occurs most often in family where
opportunities for sexual interaction are available. The absence
of the mother, for whatever reason, provides opportunities for
sexual contact between father and daughter. But this does not
mean that the mother is to blame for providing such opportunities. The mother may be absent involuntarily because of an illness that requires hospital care. Or the mother may take an extended vacation, leaving the children in the care of the father.
If the father is predisposed to form an incestuous tie with the
daughter, he may take advantage of the mother's absence to make
sexual advances while she is gone. One incest victim realls that her
mother went to visit relatives for two weeks. Prior to this, her
father had made no effort to seduce her and so she was completely
taken by suprise when he took advantage of the mother's absence
to "get me to go to bed with him." Even though her brothers
and sisters were at home during the mother's absence, her father
persisted in his efforts at seduction, "but he was careful not to
let them see him fondle my breasts or touch me all over."

In some cases, the mother is forced to take a job because her
husband is unemployed, creating an opportunity for incest to take
place. Maisch found that 34 percent of the cases in his survey
occurred while the mother was at work and the father was at
home. One incest victim recalled that the incest began when her
mother, a registered nurse, decided to work at the local hospital
during the night shift. It was during the evening that her father
would regularly begin to drink and make sexual advances to her
and to her sister. "It got to be kind of a ritual, something we just
knew was going to happen about every night when mother was

gone," she explained. "And sometimes, even if she wasn't working, she would go to bed early and leave us watching television with our father. It was almost like she was inviting us to go to bed with him, or at least that she didn't care what happened after she had gone to sleep."

Incest may also be precipitated when the mother becomes incapacitated at home. Some are suffering from fatigue or may be far along in their pregnancy, so they retire early to their rooms and leave the daughter alone with the father during the evening hours. Blair and Rita Justice cite a case in which the mother actually put the daughter in bed with the father because she couldn't tolerate the husband's snoring and decided to sleep in another room. She said her husband was lonely sleeping by himself and she put the daughter in her place with the husband.

Even though the opportunities for incest exist, most fathers are not tempted to use them to satisfy their emotional and sexual needs. The predisposing factors are already present if fathers do take advantage of such opportunities to involve daughters in sexual relationships, namely, the mother wants the daughter to take over the role of wife and mother, the father feels strongly deprived of attention and affection and the daughter is seeking approval and nurturing from her parents. Unless these conditions are present, the absence of the mother because of illness or employment is not the cause of incest; it is only one of several factors that create an environment in which an intimate relationship between father and daughter can easily develop.

REFERENCES

1. Justice, B. and Justice, R.: *The Broken Taboo*. New York, Human Sciences, 1979, p. 69.
2. Karpman, B.: Citizen Wolliam K. In Masters, R.: *Incest*. New York, Julian Press, 1963, p. 172.
3. Wells, L.: Family pathology and father-daughter incest. *J Clinical Psychiatry, 42:*197-201, 1981.
4. Maisch, H.: *Incest*. London, Andre Deutsch, 1973.
5. Ibid., p. 176.
6. Gebhard, J.: *Sex Offenders*. New York, Harper and Row, 1965.
7. Herman, J.: *Father-Daughter Incest*. Cambridge, Harvard University Press, 1981.

8. Justice and Justice, *The Broken Taboo*, p. 78.
9. Ibid., p. 63.
10. Maisch, *Incest*, p.136.
11. Herman, *Father-Daughter Incest*, p. 77.
12. Herman, J. and Hirschman, L., Father-daughter incest. In Dept. of Health and Human Resources: *Sexual Abuse of Children*, Washington, D.C., 1980, p. 71.
13. Brady, K.: *Father's Days.* New York, Seaview, 1979, p.68.
14. Herman, J.: *Father-Daughter Incest*, p.49
15. Justice and Justice, *The Broken Taboo*, p. 118.
16. Sayles, C.: Parent of a past victim. In Sanford, L.: *The Silent Children.* Garden City, New York, Anchor, 1980, p.359.
17. Maisch, *Incest*, 166.
18. Herman, *Father-Daughter Incest*, p.93.
19. Ibid., pp.109-125.
20. Ibid., p.124.
21. Maisch, *Incest*, p.177.
22. Ibid., p. 178.
23. Brady, *Father's Days*, p.55.
24. Ibid., p.65.
25. Justice and Justice, *The Broken Taboo*, p. 114.
26. Ibid., p.116.

Chapter 3

INCESTUOUS FAMILY SYSTEMS

> When family life fails,
> the inevitable consequence is
> a tendency toward dehumanization
> of behavior.
>
> Nathan Ackerman

A SENSE of security, a feeling of being accepted, valued and loved prevails in normal, healthy families. Parents are ready and able to provide for the physical and emotional needs of their children. Husbands and wives cooperate in carrying out their responsibilities and share in making important decisions. If a crisis threatens, family members unite and assist each other to cope with problems. But incestuous families are not able to withstand conflict and stress because of the personal inadequacies of individual family members and because of disturbances within the family system itself. Unable to cope with problems in an efficient and effective way, these families attempt to compensate for crippling deficiencies in functioning by developing incestuous relationships among family members. How disturbances in the family system lay the groundwork for incest will be explored in the sections that follow.

Incest as a Family Affair

The biblical account of an incestuous union between Lot and his two daughters is one of the earliest references to intra-familial sex. Believing that incest is the only way to maintain the continuity of the family, the daughters seduce their father while he is inebriated. Lot is the innocent victim of his daughters' duplicity. He would never have committed incest had he been sober, according to this account. This theme that fathers are seduced by their highly sexed and provocative daughters has persisted throughout history and is expressed in both classical literature and popular erotic writing. But the story of Lot's incestuous relation with his two daughters also contains a reasonably accurate description of a family system that is likely to produce incest. The conditions in Lot's family set the stage for the incestuous event. His wife is absent from the home, having been turned into a pillar of salt. Therefore, she is unavailable to meet her husband's sexual needs. The daughters are willing to commit incest in order for the family to survive. The father's misuse of alcohol precipitates the incest, a condition also frequently associated with sexual abuse and incestuous behavior.

In the biblical account, Lot's daughters are portrayed as being responsible for the incest, but their actions are excused because their motives were honorable. They placed the good of preserving the father's seed over the preservation of the incest taboo. But the image of the seductive daughter has persisted, even in the views of some professional clinicians who focus on the child as the principal actor in the initiation of incest. As late as 1975, Doctor James Henderson, a psychiatrist who is an authority on incest wrote: "The daughters collude in the incestuous liaison and play an active and even initiating role in establishing the pattern."[1]

The view that daughters take an active role in incest can be traced to the psychoanalytic theories of neurosis that were widely accepted in the thirties. Developed by Sigmund Freud, the psychoanalytic theory held that incest was a fantasy of women who had an unconscious desire to possess their fathers. In the course of treating middle-class female patients for symptoms of hysteria, Freud discovered that they described childhood events involving a sexual relationship with their fathers. Freud was at first convinced that his patients' accounts of incest represented an unconscious desire to replace the mother and that the events they described did not actually occur. He considered them to be sexual childhood fantasies that represented unresolved emotional and sexual feelings for their fathers. Later, Freud modified this view of the daughter's relationship to her father and concluded that many of his patients had in fact been sexually molested by their fathers.

The traditional psychoanalytic view does not provide an adequate or valid explanation of incest in the view of many social scientists and mental health workers who seek to combine individual psychodynamics with the interpersonal dynamics of the family to explain how incest develops and how incestuous relationships are maintained. They argue that incest is not the result of a neurotic disorder in the victim or a manifestation of a personality problem in an adult family member. They suggest that incest is best understood when it's regarded as a symptom of severe family dysfunctioning. Therefore, the inquiry into the causes of incestuous behavior must examine how the family system functions so as to encourage the development of certain patterns of interaction among family members. Among the areas of family functioning that are included in this examination are role definitions and role functioning, relationships among family members, distribution of power in the family structure, communication patterns and social isolation. Essentially, the incest victim is seen to be the scapegoat of the family when family functioning breaks down in one or more of these critical areas. The role of the victim is to maintain the unity of the family when the family is called upon to cope with problems that threaten to overwhelm or destroy it. Moreover, all family members are involved in condoning and supporting the incestuous behavior because it is needed to preserve the stability and unity of the family.

Mother-Daughter Role Reversal

Clinicians who have worked with incest victims and their families have noted that reversal of roles between mother and daughter is one of the most common forms of family dysfunctioning found in these family systems. Daughters take over the duties and responsibilities that mothers usually assume: the management of the household, the care and supervision of the children and looking after the needs of the father. Herman and Hirschman report that many of the daughters they interviewed had effectively replaced their mothers and became the father's surrogate wife.

They were also deputy mothers to the younger children over whom they exercised considerable authority. The position of the daughter in incestuous families is described by the authors as follows:

> While they resented being exploited and robbed of the freedom ordinarily granted dependent children, they did gain some feeling of value and importance from the role they were given. Many girls felt an enormous sense of responsibility for holding the family together. They also knew that as keepers of the incest secret, they had extraordinary power which could be used to destroy the family. Their sexual contact with their fathers conferred on them a sense of possessing a dangerous secret power over the lives of others.[2]

Blair and Rita Justice point out that the role reversal in incestuous families comes about because of the symbiotic ties between the parents and their need to have the daughter play the role of the nurturing mother. The daughter provides what the mother cannot provide, namely, love and affection for the children and the father. In these families, neither parent is autonomous. Each looks to the other to solve problems, cope with frustration and carry out the tasks related to childrearing. Each parent sees the other as someone who frustrates basic needs for nurturing. The wife perceives herself as being exploited by her husband, and the husband perceives his wife as a withholding, cold and unloving person. Therefore, it is not surprising that the mother looks to the daughter to take over the nurturing role and that the father looks to the daughter to meet his sexual needs.

Blair and Rita Justice suggest that fathers and mothers in incestuous families are pursuing the fantasy of the all-loving mother because neither parent has received adequate nurturing and care during childhood. As adults, they are trying to find a kind, all-loving mother person to compensate for the emotional deprivation they suffered in childhood. Fathers who commit incest pursue the all-loving mother fantasy when they marry a woman who they believe will meet their need for emotional and sexual gratification. But their wives turn out to have faults and are not the answer to the need for love and attention. Some wives do not choose to play the role of the "good mother" to their husbands and resent their husbands' efforts to convert them into a mother figure. Eventually, the marriage deteriorates, relationships become strained and their sexual life becomes unsatisfactory. The father then perceives the daughter as the all-loving mother and perceives the wife as the bad, rejecting mother. Thus, the psychological basis for incest has been formed.

Mothers cast their daughters in the role of the all-loving mother in incestuous families often for the same reason that fathers do they are also searching for the love and nurturing they did not receive from their own mothers. Many of them were figuratively or actually abandoned by their fathers. Their mothers were generally stern and unloving. Unhappy in their relationship with their mothers, these women usually left home at an early age, married men who mistreated them and gave them reason to reject their husbands sexually. Blair and Rita Justice point out that the deprived mother develops a hostile relationship with her own daughter because she has not been able to resolve her anger toward her own mother. "When her daughter came along, she made her into the image of her own mother. Meanwhile she continued to try to get her own mother to love her and give her the nurturing she never got as a child. The continued pursuit of the mother invariably led to more rebuffs, and only her daughter was left as any hope of offering love and nurturing."[3]

Incest victims frequently refer to the rivalry in their relationship with their mothers. Mothers also referred to a feeling that there was something wrong about the relationship between themselves and their daughters. The rivalry between them increases feelings of distrust that further impair their ability to form a close and satisfying relationship to one another. Rivalry and competition for the attention of the father is a normal part of the daughter's childhood and adolescence. Freud pointed out that the female child goes through a stage when she is strongly attracted to her father, beginning at age three and continuing to age six. Even during this early phase of her psychosexual development, the daughter is aware that her mother is her rival in competing for the love of the father. In the normal course of events, the daughter recognizes that she cannot replace her mother and turns her attention to persons outside the family. However, if the father and mother are estranged and in conflict, the daughter may learn that her father welcomes her attention and affection. She also learns that he can exploit her own need for affection and involve her in a sexual relationship for which she is not prepared.

The reversal of role between mother and daughter creates special problems because the child becomes an adult and the adult becomes a child. When generational boundaries are crossed or blurred, the strains on the family system are enormous. Children become confused because they are expected to perform far beyond their capacities. Moreover, serious damage results because children are denied the nurturing that should be forthcoming from adults. It is not surprising that incestuous families produce psychopathology in the offspring. Daughters who become victims of incest manifest a variety of psychiatric symptoms, undergo periods of severe depression or act out their emotional conflict in self-destructive behavior. These psychiatric problems reflect confusion in self-identity during the formative years of childhood and adolescence when the incestuous experience creates serious reactions of shame and guilt. The role reversal involves even more confusion about self-identity because normal childhood experiences have not been part of the victim's life. Looking back on their early lives, many women who were involved in an incestuous relation sense that they never really had a childhood because their parents thrust them into adult roles at an early age. The daughter who was expected to play the role of mother to her siblings and sex partner to her father has indeed been robbed of her childhood. She has always been asked to meet the needs of adult family members, while her own needs for nurturing have been disregarded.

Family Power Structure

All family systems contain a hierarchy of power, a pecking order that indicates how power is distributed among family members. In healthy, well-functioning families, the husband and wife have learned to share power on a fairly equal basis. Because power is shared, there is minimum disruption of relationships within the family system. The bond between the parents is highly valued by both partners, and they arrive at decisions based on a careful consideration of what is in the best interests of all family members. The parents do not exercise their authority capriciously or arbitrarily. They negotiate differences and share in making important decisions that affect the life of the family.

The power structure of incestuous families is quite different. Studies indicate that power is highly concentrated in the father and that he holds a dominant position in families where incest occurs. He intimidates and controls other family members. Maisch found that in an overwhelming majority of incest cases, the family was subjected to the domineering influence of the husband and father. In some instances, the father resorts to the use of force and violence to maintain control over the family. Herman found that half the informants reported that their fathers were habitually violent and that they had seen their fathers beat their mothers.[4]

The unequal distribution of power, the complete dominance of the father, is one of the chief factors that leads to father-daughter incest. When other family members have little or no power, the father can exploit his daughter without encountering resistance from other family members. If his authority goes unchallenged (if the mother has no power or authority), the daughter is extremely vulnerable because she cannot rely on other family members to protect her against the father's demands for sexual gratification. The mother's powerlessness in the face of the father's tyrannical rule is one of the factors that lay the groundwork for incest to occur. "As long as fathers rule but do not nurture, as long as mothers nurture but do not rule, the conditions favoring father-daughter incest will prevail," writes Herman. "Only a basic change in power relations of mothers and fathers can prevent the sexual exploitation of children."[5]

The development of an incestuous relationship with the father places the daughter in a special position in the power structure. She can lay claim to some degree of power because she holds "the secret" and uses it in gaining favors from the father. Although the father can use his power to give or withhold material gifts and special privileges, the daughter can withhold or grant sexual favors. However, the daughter's power is no match for the father's power. Perceiving that he is the most powerful family member, the daughter soon recognizes that her survival depends on pleasing

Slavery

him or offering minimum resistance to him until she is old enough and strong enough to make it on her own. She also begins to recognize that her mother is powerless and that she cannot look to her mother to interfere in the incestuous behavior of the father, a fact that becomes painfully obvious if she tells her mother what is happening and finds that her mother cannot do anything to stop the incest.

The power of the father and his demand for sexual favors from his daughter derives from the commonly held view that the male is superior to the female and that his authority is indisputable. Once the father is perceived to be superior to his wife and his daughter, he is automatically endowed with the right to rule over them and to control and exploit them for his own purposes. As head of the family, his decisions are taken to be final and his actions are not to be questioned by other family members. His wife and his children are his possessions and what he does within the privacy of his home is not a concern of others. Within this framework of cultural values, the wife and daughter are subject to sexual as well as physical abuse. Feminists argue that a patriarchal family system encourages father-daughter incest for these reasons. "As long as fathers dominate their faimiles," writes Herman, "they will have the power to make sexual use of their children. Most fathers will choose not to exercise this power, but as long as the prerogative is implicitly granted to all men, some men will use it."[6]

The patriarchal family view has a strong impact on daughters who become victims of incest. Many of them admire the masculine image that their fathers project in contrast to the weak and ineffectual women they married. The daughters also note that male children fare much better than their female counterparts. Their brothers are given more freedom and privileges and are usually excused from household chores. In contrast, the father exercises minute control over the females in the family. He even restricts the activites of his wife and daughters to the extent of confining them to the home.

Victims of father-daughter incest also report that their fathers actively discouraged social contacts and isolated them from the outside world. Fathers generally criticized their daughters' boyfriends, constantly questioned them about their sexual encounters and inquired into their private affairs. By extending their control over every aspect of their daughters' lives, incestuous fathers insured complete control over the family. By preventing the daughter from making social contacts, the father also insures that the incestuous relationship will be maintained and remain undiscovered and he can continue to use her sexually without fear of exposure.

Some psychoanalysts argue that the power accorded to men in a patriarchal society is recognized by the female child in early childhood. Even at a very early age, she discovers that males are preferred to females. Later, the daughter begins to turn to the father with attempts to please him in the hope that he will confer on her some of the power that is accorded to the male sex. One way in which she can gain the father's favor and participate more fully in the family power structure is to form an intimate tie with him. If the father takes advantage of the daughter's hope to gain power through a sexual relationship with him, he may find that she does not actively resist his sexual advances. Phyllis Chesler, a feminist psychologist, make this point when she writes: "Women are encouraged to commit incest as a way of life. As opposed to marrying our fathers, we marry men like our fathers, men who are older than us, have more money than us, more power than us, are taller than us — our fathers." For some victims, incest may seem to be the only path to power, but too often it provides only the appearance of power and the price is much too high.

The Marital Relationship

Clinicians who have worked with incest victims' families have noted that serious marital problems are frequently associated with father-daughter incest. Maisch reported that husbands and wives were experiencing sexually and emotionally disturbed relationships in 80 percent of all cases of father-daughter incest and concluded that marital dissatisfaction was one of the principal factors leading to incest. Arguments over money, differences about childrearing practices and other problems in daily living go unresolved and increase the couple's feelings of hostility and frustration. Marital partners sometimes act out their hostility in frequent episodes of violence, but in many families, the husband and wife express their anger through long periods of silence and avoidance. It is during these periods of conflict or withdrawal that the father uses the daughter as a source of comfort and turns to her for companionship and affection to relieve the stress resulting from the marital conflict. Trying to make her father's life more pleasant, the daughter eventually accepts his sexual advances to make him happy. As Maisch points out, the process of drifting into an incestuous relationship is frequently due to an unhappy marital relation that prepares the ground for the father's attempt to seduce the daughter. Both the father and the daughter attempt to overcome the problems in the marriage by escaping into an incestuous relationship. The daughter functions as a stabilizing influence in the family and helps the marital partners remain in the relationship. She takes on the responsibility for meeting the father's needs, which becomes essential to maintaining the family through her nurturing role.

Studies of father-daughter incest frequently refer to sexual difficulties between the parents as one of the characteristics of these families. Maisch reported that 52 percent of the fathers involved in incest with their daughters had an unsatisfactory sex relation with their wives. Victims also often state that their father turned to them for sexual gratification because the mother was frigid. The statements of incest offenders are usually self-serving. Both the victim and the perpetrator can rationalize the incest as being a by-product of sexual frustration. However, researchers point out that incest presents a unique solution to the problem of sexual frustration due to the wife's lack of interest in sex. The husband might turn to someone outside the family for sexual gratification or divorce his wife. But these men do not leave their wives or engage in extramarital sex. Incestuous fathers offer several explanations. Some say that they regard incest as less sinful than adultery. Others believe that the daughter is a legitimate object for sexual outlet. The majority of incestuous fathers explain that they are merely expressing affection for their daughters and that the sexual relationship grows out of a need for approval and attention that is not met by their wives. Katherine

Brady recalls that her father told her he could not make love to another woman unless he felt affection for her and suggested that only Katherine could fill his emotional and sexual needs.

Family therapists point out that incestuous families are characteristically closed family systems in which family members are closely intertwined into what Murray Bowen calls an "undifferentiated ego mass." In such families, the boundaries between members are never clearly delineated. The sense of individuality and autonomy that is essential to personal growth is lacking because of the highly symbiotic nature of the relationship among family members. Therefore, all the needs of family members must be met within the family. These closed family systems are also shut off from outside influences and from resources that could provide opportunities for personal satisfaction and growth. The family sets boundaries around the family system and these boundaries are impenetrable. Because of strong ties of mutual dependence, family members must look to one another for support. These are the conditions under which incestuous relationships begin to develop and are maintained.

Victims as Scapegoats

The daughter who becomes the victim of incest is the family scapegoat. By displacing their problems on the daughter, the parents maintain their marriage intact at the expense of the daughter's normal emotional development. In the role of family scapegoat, the daughter keeps the family intact at the cost of sacrificing herself. Family therapists point out that the scapegoat is used by the family to divert attention from underlying conflict and problems that the family is not able to resolve. For example, the sexual alienation of the marital partners threatens the continuation of the marriage. The father and mother are unable to come to a resolution of the sexual problems and the daughter is then used to avoid the necessity of dealing with the marital difficulty. In many families, the parents blame the daughter for the problems that they are unable to resolve. They describe the daughter as a troublemaker and suggest that she was responsible for initiating the incestuous relationship with her father. Both parents may accuse her of being provocative and seductive, a "bad" girl who deliberately set about creating problems for the family.

The scapegoating process reflects the inability of the adult family members to take responsibility for the incest. Blair and Rita Justice point out that parents in abusing families are unable to protect the child from harm because they are tied into a relationship of mutual dependency that does not allow one parent to restrain the other from causing injury and mistreatment of the child. Therefore, the abuse continues without interference from either parent. When confronted with a problem, the father and mother find ways of discounting the need to deal with it and adopt a stance of passivity that enables them to avoid seeking a solution. Discounting takes one of four forms: denying that the problem exists; discounting the significance of the problem; defining the problem as insolvable; blaming the problem on the child.

The discounting process is found in most incestuous families. In many cases, the mother is aware of the fact that the father is sexually misusing the daughter but makes no effort to stop the incest. Therapists have been surprised to find cases in which the incestuous relationship has been maintained for years despite the fact that the mother had many opportunities to observe the father's behavior. Victims report that they sensed their mothers "knew that something was wrong," but the daughters also sensed that their mothers did not want to know that the "something wrong" was incest. Many daughters actually protect their mothers from knowing the truth and continue to remain in the role of the family scapegoat. Katherine Brady explains:

> From the beginning I felt the impulse to tell Mother, but always it was overruled by that passive needy part of me which couldn't risk losing her approval. I knew she would believe it was my fault. She'd told me I caused things when I sat on Dad's lap. I knew only that I must try to please my parents in whatever way they prescribed. By so doing keep peace in the house, satisfy my instatiable need for endorsement.[7]

As family scapegoat, the daughter faces a dilemma. If she discloses the family incest secret, she will be held responsible for causing the family to fall apart. If she chooses to remain silent, she will be accused of encouraging the continuation of the incestuous relationship and contributing to the family's perception of her as a bad child. The messages that the daughter receives from her father reinforce her need to remain in the role of the family scapegoat. He tells her that she is attractive and that she is the only person in the world who understands him and can make him happy. But he also warns her that she must never disclose this wonderful relation between them to anyone because disaster will follow. The family will be destroyed, the mother will be devastated and he will be sent to prison. Yet, the father tells her that there is nothing wrong about the incestuous relationship and that their sexual activity is a normal and natural expression of love between fathers and daughters.

These contradictory messages leave the daughter in a state of extreme confusion. She is told that there is nothing abnormal about incest, but she is also told never to disclose the secret relationship. Laing, a British family therapist, uses the term *mystification* to describe how some families use communication to obscure or mask what is happening within the family system. Family members can use mystification to cloud over incest. The father uses it to confuse the daughter. She is made to feel that she is behaving wrongfully but that her father wants her to continue to carry on the relationship and remain silent about it. She is caught in a double bind. If she reveals the secret, she will have disobeyed her father's instructions. If she does not reveal the secret, she must continue in the wrongful behavior. No matter which course she chooses, she will have to pay a price. Confronted with this choice, many daughters choose to remain silent. Even as adults, they keep the secret and play out the role of the family scapegoat long after the incest has stopped.

Social Isolation

Incestuous families are generally found to be socially isolated. In most cases, strict and impermeable boundaries between the family and the outside world are erected as a barrier to socialization with other persons. Self-contained and removed from the normal experiences of interaction with others, family members ·

do not benefit from the stimulation of exchanging ideas, values or experiences with persons outside the family. When families become detached from the outside world, they deteriorate and develop various forms of pathology. One form of pathology that may develop as a result of social isolation is incest because family members have no support system that enables them to cope with stress and meet their needs. When family members are dependent on just one person in the family to gain affection and nurturing, the possibility of incest increases. If the family system is open to outside contacts, the possibility is decreased because there are multiple sources of support available when they are needed, and family members are less dependent on each other for gratification of essential needs, for nurturing, affection and personal fulfillment.

Not only does social isolation contribute to the development of incest, it is also an important factor in maintaining the incestuous relationship once it has been established. The victim of incest is effectively shut off from normal social relationships with others. Children who live in an incestuous family tend not to form friendships with peers because they sense that they are different in significant ways from other children. Girls who are involved in an incestuous relationship do not dare to talk with other girls about their families. They cannot share in the experiences of other girls who have a normal nonincestuous relationship to their fathers. One victim of father-daughter incest described her feelings about her relationship to girls her age: "I didn't get along with other girls. I felt older than them. For one thing, I'd been into sex since eight years old, and when I knew that, I felt different."

Another victim recalls that she felt uniquely different from others and could never relate to her peers in a normal way during her childhood: "I would go to school feeling, 'Shit, nobody else in the world has gone through what I've gone through. Nobody else knows anything about this sort of thing. Nobody imagines or else they would be able to talk on this kind of level.' And nobody could."

The social isolation of the incest victim is also imposed on her by her father who discourages her from having social contacts. Boyfriends are not welcome. There are no planned occasions for her to invite others to her home. Feelings of suspicion and distrust of other people are constantly brought home to daughters who are involved in an incestuous relationship when fathers warn them about intimate relationships with boys. In such an environment, the incestuous behavior can continue without the knowledge or interference of persons outside the family.

Sexual Climate

The sexual climate of the home is an important factor in the development of incest. Studies of incestuous families indicate that the children often undergo experiences that are highly erotic. Children become confused about appropriate sexual behavior and become vulnerable to sexual exploitation by family members. Mothers may contribute to the development of father-daughter incest inadvertently. A fifteen-year-old girl recalled that she wanted to have underpants that had the days of the week imprinted on them. "The next thing I knew," she recalls, "my father went out and bought them. He gave them to me and asked me to model them. My mother thought it was real cute." Another victim recalled that her father took her shopping to buy a training bra because her mother was too busy to go with her. When one daughter was approaching puberty, she became worried because one of her breasts was developing more rapidly than the other. She told her mother about her concern. The mother told her to show her father what was happening because he could explain it better.

Weinberg found that the families included in his study of incest had very permissive attitudes toward sex. Children routinely observed their parents having sexual intercourse and often slept with their parents in the same bed. Parents showed their children pornographic materials and used obscene language freely. But sexual stimulation of children in the family usually takes more subtle forms, such as playful romping that leads to more overt forms of sexual play including sexual kissing and bodily caressing. The line between normal forms of expression of affection between parent and child as distinguished from sexual contacts is sometimes unclear, but when the parent uses the child to fulfill the need for sexual stimulation, the possibility of incest increases.

Complete suppression of sexual interest and feelings is also

associated with incest. Victims report that they never heard sexual matters discussed by their parents and that they were never permitted to see their parents undress. Bathroom doors were carefully locked when a parent was taking a shower. Television shows that hinted at sexual encounters were strictly forbidden. In an environment that strictly prohibits any interest in sex, the child grows up curious and uninformed, without the knowledge that is needed to prevent the possibility of sexual exploitation by an adult. It comes as no surprise that father-daughter incest can occur in families that outwardly appear to be highly "nonsexual."

Early studies of incest placed considerable importance on physical overcrowding as a contributing factor in the development of intimate relations among family members. It was thought that the close contact between family members exposed the children to sexual contacts if separate bedroom facilities were not available due to cramped living quarters or because of inappropriate sleeping arrangements. However, it is now believed that parents do not sleep in the same bed with children because of limited space. Fathers usually manufacture a reason to invite the child into sleeping with them, and some mothers encourage this arrangement even if it is not really necessary. Weinberg's study showed that more than half of the families included in the sample were living in substandard or overcrowded housing, but in only two cases could the overcrowding have been a reason for the father and daughter sleeping together. The deciding factor appears to be the motivation of the parents, rather than the physical environment, in the development of incest. If the family members do not attempt to satisfy their sexual needs through the child, the physical environment will have little effect on the likelihood of incest.

Profile of Incestuous Families

Although no one factor or combination of factors is present in every incestuous family system, deficiences in specific areas of functioning are found in all cases of father-daughter incest. The profile of incestuous families that follows indicates significant differences between healthy family systems and incestuous family systems. In general, the following deficiencies are characteristic of families in which father-daughter incest occurs:

LACK OF A STRONG COALITION BETWEEN THE PAR-
ENTS. Parents work cooperatively to provide leadership for the
family in healthy families. Incestuous families are troubled by division and conflict between the marital partners, ties between husband and wife are weak, and both feel alienated and lonely.

MOTHERS ARE PHYSICALLY OR PSYCHOLOGICALLY
ABSENT. In healthy families, both parents provide optimal care
and nurturing for the children, and relationships among family
members are characterized by strong bonds of affection. In incestuous families, mothers are remote and tend to be alienated from
the children. Mothers in these families feel inadequate in meeting
the responsibility of the nurturing role and compensate by becoming totally absorbed in work and other activities from which they
gain personal satisfaction.

MOTHER-DAUGHTER ROLES ARE REVERSED. Genera-
tional boundaries are clearly defined in healthy families. Adult
family members do not permit children to cross these generational
boundaries. In incestuous families, daughters assume the role of
mother, and the relation between the mother and the daughter is
inappropriately structured. Both parents perceive the child as an
adult, and family roles are seriously distorted.

POWER IS UNEQUALLY DISTRIBUTED BETWEEN HUS-
BAND AND WIFE. Marital partners share power in healthy families, and decisions are arrived at by mutual consent. Wives in healthy
families have a partnership relationship with their husbands, but
wives in incestuous families are submissive. Incestuous fathers hold
a position of power that enables them to control all aspects of
their partners' lives as well as the lives of the children. Decisions
are made by the father without consultation with the mother.

CONFLICT IS RESOLVED THROUGH SCAPEGOATING.
Healthy families resolve conflict through communication and negotiation of difference. Incestuous families avoid open confrontation of conflict and resolve problems by scapegoating the incest
victim. The scapegoat is used by the marital pair to obscure severe
problems in their relationship. The incestuous relationship serves
to maintain the marriage but results in damaging the victim.

FAMILY AFFECT IS NOT SUPPORTIVE TO FAMILY

MEMBERS. Healthy family systems are characterized by strong bonds of mutual support that create an environment conducive to optimal functioning of all family members. Such supportive relations are absent in incestuous families. Members exploit one another. Sexual contacts are confused with or equated with genuine expressions of affection and nurturing.

FAMILY MEMBERS LACK AUTONOMY. Healthy families encourage members to achieve a high level of autonomy and self-confidence. Each family member has a strong sense of self-identity and individuality. Incestuous family systems create symbiotic ties among family members that restrict development of autonomy, result in low self-esteem and prohibit personal growth of family members.

COMMUNICATION IS CONFUSED. Healthy families use communication effectively to resolve problems and work out difficulties in relationships among family members. Incestuous families have difficulty in communicating clearly, expressing feelings and resolving problems through negotiation of differences. Messages are ambiguous and often inconsistent, contributing to confusion and disorganization of the family system.

FAMILY MEMBERS ARE SOCIALLY ISOLATED. Healthy families are open family systems that encourage interaction and socialization with persons outside the family system. Incestuous families actively discourage contact with persons outside the family, and family members depend entirely on other family members to meet their needs. Without input from the external environment and social network, the possibility of personal growth is restricted.

THE FAMILY IS UNABLE TO COPE WITH STRESS. Healthy family systems demonstrate an ability to deal with problems as they arise, and the unity of the family is not threatened in time of crisis. Incestuous families are weakened by internal conflict, alienation and ineffective communication. Therefore, they are extremely vulnerable and the ability of the family to cope with crisis situations is seriously undermined.

The following case history of a victim of multiple incest illustrates how a dysfunctional family system can create the conditions under which incestuous relations develop and continue over a period of several years.

Alice

When Alice was two years old her mother attempted to kill her. Symptoms of a severe mental illness had been observed prior to this traumatic incident, and the mother was committed to a psychiatric hospital for treatment. Soon thereafter, Alice, her father and her siblings made their home with the paternal grandparents who lived on a small farm in the Southwest. Alice recalls that her grandparents had no contacts with neighbors and that the family was socially isolated from other people in the small rural community.

Alice and her brother were physically and sexually abused by their grandfather. The grandmother was aware that the grandfather was abusive, but she made no effort to interfere. Alice's father worked in a nearby town and was away from the home when the abuse was taking place. Alice's earliest recollections about sexual abuse go back to age three, involving her grandfather who engaged her in sexual contacts when she was still very young. One time he tried to rape her in an open field. When she was about five years old, he made another attempt to force her to have sexual intercourse. Alice described what happened. "I used to go to the barn to play with my dolls and get away from my grandfather. But this time he followed me into the barn and barred the door. Then I remember he dragged me up into the hayloft. I tried to get away and, in the scuffle, I fell down outside the barn onto the ground below. I remember that I must have been unconscious after I fell. My grandmother came running out of the house and thought I was dead. Later, my grandfather whipped me for being disobedient and told me I should not have been playing in the barn."

Life with her grandparents left Alice totally isolated from other people, except during the fall and spring when she looked forward to going to school — a welcome relief from the abuse she suffered daily. But at school Alice had few friends. She recalls that she thought she was different from other children. "Everybody else was prettier, everybody else was smarter," Alice said. "That is the way I felt. And I couldn't share what was happening to me with anyone else. I don't remember much about what kind of clothes I wore, but I do remember that I had a pair

of overalls that I liked because they were nice and soft and I knew
my grandfather couldn't get into them and put his hands between
my legs. I never did like dresses, and I still don't like to wear them
because they make me feel clumsy. I feel very uncomfortable
when I try to look feminine."

When she was growing up, Alice always wondered what a real
family would be like, "a place that wasn't so scary" as she described it. When she was age six, Alice's father remarried, but the
new wife was not the ideal mother that Alice longed for in her
fantasies of a happy family. Alice's stepmother was moody and depressed most of the time. "We left her alone when she was depressed, and then when she got ready she would come out of it
and for awhile we would have a pretty good time," Alice recalls.
The father's second marriage was not a happy one. There were
many problems; Alice remembers that her father vented his anger
on her and her younger brother. Sometimes he became violent and
abusive. The marriage lasted six years, and it was during this period in her life that Alice was sexually assaulted by a sixteen-year-
old male cousin who lived with the family. The cousin's sexual assaults were psychologically and physically traumatic experiences
for Alice. She was forced into sexual intercourse and there were
obvious indications of vaginal bleeding as a result of the forced
penetration. When Alice tried to explain to her stepmother why
she was bleeding, the stepmother gave Alice sanitary napkins to
absorb the blood and told her that she was just beginning to men-
struate earlier than most girls.

After her father and stepmother separated, Alice went to live
with her maternal aunt during the summer. Here she again became the victim of incest. "There was an uncle who lived with my
aunt," Alice relates. "He would come into the room while I was
watching television. I remember I was lying on the floor when he
came in and laid down beside me. Then he started feeling me up,
fondling my breasts and wanted to have sex with me. But he
really wasn't very forceful and I was able to fight him off."

At the end of the summer, Alice's father married again. This
marriage lasted only a few months and again the father grew rest-
less. But he told Alice that he only married in order that she
would have a mother to take care of her. When the marriages did

not turn out well, Alice would be blamed because "I was always giving his wife a rough time." Her father was married to eight different women. Each of these marriages ended after bitter and violent conflict, and Alice was not accepted by any of the women whom her father married. After a very unsuccessful marriage, Alice's father would move to a new city, taking the children with him. "We never stayed in one place long enough to establish any friendships," Alice said. "He would always make such a dramatic thing out of moving when things didn't go right and he couldn't take it any longer. We were never allowed to tell our friends at school good-bye. We were told to behave as if nothing had happened and not tell anybody where we were going. Then we would move on to another place, once to Colorado and once to California. But then we would never stay there very long either."

When Alice was fourteen years old, her father's sixth marriage ended in divorce, and she began to take over most of the housekeeping duties, prepared the meals and even took over the management of the family's finances. Her father changed occupations and began to drink heavily. He joined a motorcycle club and used drugs. Alice remembers that her father was very unhappy at this point in his life. He began to look to Alice for sympathy and emotional support. "At first I felt sorry for him when he would cry and tell me how much he needed me," Alice recalled. "I was just the age of my mother when she married my father and I guess he thought of me in that way, sort of like his wife. And I was really very well developed by that time. Maybe that had something to do with it. Or maybe I reminded him of himself when he was young. But he began to act in ways I didn't like when he was around me. At first it was sexual kissing, and he would hold me tight against him when he did it. Then one time he wanted to have sex with me. He kept following me around and I knew what would happen; so I turned around and slapped him. After that, he never bothered me again. But I never trusted him after that. I thought to myself: 'Don't be stupid and ever let yourself be caught with him alone'."

Alice's experience of sexual abuse by her grandfather, her uncle, her cousin and her father illustrates how a very disturbed family system lays the groundwork for sexual exploitation of the child. The absence of a kind and loving mother was an important factor that contributed to the sexual abuse. From early childhood, Alice had no mother surrogate to whom she could turn for affection or protection. Her grandmother was remote and inaccessible, leaving Alice without a source of help when her grandfather began to molest her at the age of three. The father's frequent moves from one city to another added to the instability of the family. During most of her childhood, Alice had no permanent roots or normal family life. None of the women her father married accepted her or gave her the attention and affection she needed in order to develop a feeling of belonging. Without strong family ties and a supportive network, Alice was isolated, insecure and extremely vulnerable to sexual exploitation.

The father's inability to make satisfactory social adjustments to work and marriage was also an important factor in the development of incest in Alice's family. She recalls that her father frequently expressed feelings of failure and dissatisfaction with his work. In an attempt to solve his problems, he would impulsively quit his job and move to another city, placing severe stress on the family because of the constant changes to which they had to accommodate. The instability of the family was also the result of the father's frequent marriages, all of which ended in more frustration, disillusionment and eventually an abrupt termination of the relationship. As in most incestuous families, the marital bonds were extremely weak, the relation between the father and the women he married was marked by conflict and upheaval, providing little security for Alice and her brother as he moved from one marital partner to another.

The absence of a strong supportive woman in Alice's life is also an important factor in explaining why she was subjected to sexual abuse throughout her childhood. Her grandmother did not protect her when her grandfather molested her. Her stepmother did not intervene when her cousin assaulted her. As Alice explained: "I kept thinking that if any of them knew what was happening, they would protect me. And justice would be served. But they did nothing. My father, my grandmother, my stepmother, they did nothing to stop it." As in other cases of incest, family members denied that the sexual abuse was taking place or minimized the significance of the problem. The inability or unwillingness of the grandmother and the stepmother to come to Alice's defense indicates how the passivity of adult family members produces an environment in which sexual abuse, as well as physical abuse, can develop and be maintained.

The social isolation of Alice's family was also an important factor in maintaining the incestuous behavior. "We lived out in this little farm house," Alice recalled. "My grandfather hadn't worked since the Depression. My father worked in a nearby town, and when he wasn't working he was out 'socializing.' There were no other people around when all these things took place." So the abuse went on undiscovered by persons outside the family. "I always had scars from being abused," Alice said. "But they were always covered up when I went to school so nobody knew what was happening. And I didn't dare tell anyone about it either."

As happens in many incestuous families, Alice became a substitute wife for her father in early adolescence. In the absence of a mother, she took over the responsibilities of running the household. She also became her father's confidante and was a source of comfort and support for him when he felt discouraged or disappointed. The relationship between Alice and her father was, in her own words, "emotional incest." But it became an erotic relationship when he began to see in Alice a woman who could meet his sexual needs as well as his emotional needs. By this time, Alice had developed into a sexually attractive teenager, and her emerging sexuality was not lost on her father. Studies show that this stage in the biological development of the daughter can precipitate sexual advances from the father who sees in her the fulfillment of his sexual fantasies, an opportunity to reaffirm his sexual virility and gain back his self-esteem. Such was the case with Alice's father. By this time, he had turned to hard drugs in addition to alcohol in order to cope with stress and frustration. His capacity to deal with problems was limited, and he had exhausted his personal resources. He looked to his daughter to provide emotional support and gradually he looked to her to fill his sexual needs also.

Psychodynamics of Incest

The psychodynamics of incest follow a fairly well-defined

pattern of interactions between three key family members: the father, the mother and the daughter. Each of these individuals plays a role in the development of the incestuous relationship. The father is often a person who seems quite well adjusted and functions adequately in most areas. The breakdown occurs only when roles within the family become disturbed at some specific point in the life of the family. The role distortion in the father is often a flight from a stressful and disappointing life situation. The male menopause is such a period in the lives of many men who seek to affirm their masculine virility in love affairs with younger women. The incestuous father differs in that he is inhibited, more rigidly devoted to his role as a family man and determined to fulfill his sexual needs within the marriage. However, if his wife does not fulfill his sexual needs and fantasies, he turns to his daughter to relieve his frustration and to help him regain his sense of masculinity.

The wife of the incestuous father is typically a woman who is disenchanted with her husband and is no longer interested in satisfying her husband's need to reaffirm his sexuality. She is often resentful of her adolescent daughter's sexual attractiveness and may hold back her social development when the daughter reaches puberty. The wife sometimes turns to interests outside the family to fulfill her own needs for personal fulfillment. Away from home much of the time, she counts on her daughter to take her place.

The daughter is the third corner of the incestuous triangle. As she enters womanhood, she looks to her mother as a model of femininity and then tests out her own femininity on her father. If the father feels that he needs sexual stimulation that the adolescent girl provides, he may respond to the daughter's growing sexual attractiveness and gradually relate to her as a wife instead of as a daughter. The daughter is initially pleased by the attention that she receives from her father and is inclined to accept his open displays of affection. She does not refuse her father's sexual advances and does not have enough experience to know where to draw the line. She depends on her father to set limits, but if he persists in wanting to press her into intimate sexual relations, she usually tries to protest. Despite his daughter's protests, the father may continue his harassment and eventually his sexual arousal may overcome his good judgment. He fails to carry out his protective role as a parent. The daughter then feels that she has been betrayed by her father.

If the daughter tries to escape from the incestuous relation and turns to her mother to protect her, the mother may accuse her of lying or charge her with seducing the father. If the mother accepts the story, she may refuse to take effective action to stop the incest. Some mothers tell their daughters that if the secret is revealed the father will be sent to prison and the family will be destroyed. If the mother confronts the father with the daughter's charges, he will usually deny that the incest has taken place. If the case comes to trial, the mother may prevail on the daughter to change her testimony in order to avoid exposure and disgrace. Or the father may be acquitted and the court may order the daughter to be placed in foster care. As a result, the daughter may come to believe that she is responsible for breaking up the family and even for the incest itself.

Summit and Kryso point out that, even if the secret is contained within the family, the daughter's life is significantly changed by the incestuous experience. Because the father abdicates his role as a parent, relationships within the family become confused.

> The father abdicates his authority along with his parental responsibility. There is a struggle for power in which the girl exploits her position to demand favors and avoid parental limits. With this inversion of roles, there is no hope of normal discipline and guidance. The father tries to be superauthoritarian in one area: limiting his daughter's access to potential boyfriends and outside contacts.[8]

The possibility of incest is present in almost every family. When people live together over an extended period of time, depend on each other for love and emotional support and have daily intimate contact, they tend to develop sexual feelings toward one another. However, in most families fathers are not inclined to engage in sexual relations with their daughters. Even though the feeling of sexual attraction is present, most fathers recognize that as a parent they are responsible for preventing an

incestuous relationship from developing. Under most circumstances, the father remains in control of his behavior. But if he
is facing a stressful situation such as sexual estrangement from his
wife, if he begins to drink and if he is at home alone with his
daughter, he may cross the line to commit incest. The lack of impulse control is one of the critical factors in this regard. If he is
highly impulsive, the father will turn to his daugther to solve his
problems or relieve his discomfort by gratifying his sexual needs.
But if he is in control of his impulses, the father will not turn to
his daughter and involve her in a sexual relationship, even in a
stressful situation. He will find other ways to solve his problems
and seek other outlets for coping with stress.

Researchers and clinicians have also called attention to role
confusion within the family as a critical factor in the development of incest. Because of excessively strong desires to have their
emotional needs satisfied, adult family members look to their
children to take on adult roles for which they are not prepared
and cannot possibly perform. The role reversal between daughters
and mothers is an example of what occurs when adult roles and
child roles are confused. The child is perceived as a surrogate figure for some other person. Fathers who become involved in an
incestuous relationship with their daughters see them as adults
and as appropriate objects for fulfilling adult needs, without regard to whether such expectations are appropriate. Sanford points
out the difference between the incestuous family and most American families. "In most American families," she writes, "the rights
and priveleges of adults are clearly delineated from the rights and
priveleges of children. Adults look to each other for support and
guidance . . . And if things go wrong, it is not the child's responsibility to make it up to the adult." Sanford goes on to point out
that such is not the case in incestuous families. "Every family
member is on the same shaky footing," she writes. "None of
them are sure of who they are or how they fit into the rest of
the world. Because they have so little going for them outside
the family, the children are responsible for the parent's happiness. In a sense, the child exists to nurture the parent. The parent,
feeling emotionally bankrupt, has little to offer the child."[9]

REFERENCES

1. Henderson, J.: Incest. In Freedman, A.: *Comprehensive Textbook of Psychiatry*. Baltimore, Williams and Wilkins, 1975, p. 1536.
2. Herman, J., and Hirschman, L.: Father-daughter incest. In Department of Human Services. *Sexual Abuse of Children*. Washington, D.C., 1980, p. 71.
3. Justice, B., and Justice, R.: *The Broken Taboo*. New York, Human Sciences, 1979, p. 147.
4. Herman, J.: *Father-Daughter Incest*. Cambridge, Mass., Harvard U., 1981, p. 73.
5. Ibid., p. 206.
6. Ibid.
7. Brady, K.: *Father's Days*. New York, Seaview, 1979, p. 144.
8. Summit, R., and Kryso, J.: Sexual abuse of children. In U.S. Department of Human Resources: *Sexual Abuse of Children*. Washington, D.C., 1980, p. 52.
9. Sanford, L.: *The Silent Children*. Garden City, New York, Anchor, 1980, p. 155.

Chapter 4

HELPING VICTIMS AND
THEIR FAMILIES

Opening the secret opens other
doors, too. Now we can talk to
each other without the secret
pushing us away from each other.

An incest victim

BECAUSE incest has such severely devastating effects, immediate intervention is urgently needed to help victims and their
families cope with the crisis. When the secret is discovered, family
relationships are disrupted, creating serious problems that require
attention from social workers and mental health personnel. To
enable the family to cope with the problems that accompany
disclosure of an incestuous relationship, communities provide
individual counseling for children, adolescents and adult family
members. In addition, group-therapy programs have been established for victims and for their parents. Some communities have
also developed family therapy as a method for helping families
explore why incest occurred and how they can prevent it from
happening again. The sections that follow describe these approaches to helping incest victims and their families.

Helping the Abused Children

Helping a child who has been sexually abused is a difficult
but important undertaking. Effective helping is based on a careful analysis of the nature of the incest, an assessment of the impact on the child and the development of a coordinated treatment

approach. The helping process focuses on one or more of the following areas: (1) the damaged-goods syndrome; (2) guilt feelings associated with the incest; (3) fear of the consequences of the incest experience; (4) symptoms of depression related to the disclosure of the incest; (5) repressed anger and hostility toward the offender; and (6) difficulty in developing trusting relationships.

Usually no physical injury or impairment results from the sexual abuse, but the child may have experienced pain during the sexual activity and conclude that serious injury occurred. Adolescent girls who have been incest victims often fear that they have been damaged and that they cannot grow up normally or cannot have children. Helping victims deal with these fears through support and reassurance is an important component of treatment. The victim and the family can be assured that the medical examination shows that no lasting damage has been done and eliminate the suspicion that "something might be wrong."

Because society regards sexual experience as an adult prerogative, the victim is sometimes considered to have been altered by the incestuous experience and that she is no longer a child. Histories of incest victims reveal that once the child has been subjected to sexual abuse, she is regarded as "fair game" and is victimized by a succession of sexual assaults by other family members or adults who have learned about the incest. Therefore, parents need to understand that the victim must be viewed as a child, not as an adult. She has not been transformed or achieved adult status because she underwent a sexual experience.

Incest victims have strong feelings of guilt about their part in the sexual activity and believe that they were responsible for participating in incestuous behavior. It is important that this faulty perception not be reinforced by adults in the child's environment. Some children come to feel guilty about having revealed that incest was taking place, especially if the disclosure results in divorce or separation or imprisonment of the father. Helping the victim identify guilt reactions is the first step in treatment. The therapist makes it clear to the child and to the family that no child can be held responsible for initiating sexual activity with an adult or blamed for the disruption that follows disclosure. The victim is assured that the offender is the only one who can be held accountable for the development of incestuous behavior, and the offender is the person who is responsible for the disruption of the family.

Some children fear reprisal after disclosure. Their fears are manifested in sleep disturbances and frightening dreams related to sexual abuse. Dreams usually reflect fears of separation in which the child is kidnapped by unknown persons while she is walking home from school, or dreams involve a repetition of the incest experience. Measures are taken to relieve the child's anxiety by making sure that the home environment is safe and that there is a responsible adult present to protect the child against harm or sexual abuse.

Children who have been sexually abused usually manifest symptoms of depression. The depression may be masked by complaints of fatigue or take the form of acting out through mutilation or suicide attempts. All incest victims are troubled by low self-esteem combined with a feeling that they have been spoiled or damaged by the incest. Their self-confidence has also been undermined if they have grown up in families where contact with peers was restricted. Therefore, they have limited social skills and find it difficult to relate to children of the same age. Group therapy is effective in helping them deal with this aspect of their lives because they derive support from other group members and gain a higher level of self-esteem.

Although some children appear outwardly calm, many are inwardly angry at the persons who abused them and with the family member who failed to protect them. The child's feelings toward the father in cases of father-daughter incest are often both positive and negative. This feeling toward the father may be colored by the fact that he provided nurturing and also gave the child material gifts. One eighteen-year-old girl said that her stepfather really cared for her and she still expressed affection for him. "I loved my stepfather," she said. "For two years I considered him my lover. He bought me beautiful things like a diamond ring and a car." Such positive expressions of affection are rather rare. In some cases the child has not only been sexually abused but has also been subjected to physical mistreatment by the father or stepfather. One victim recalled that she had lived in the same house with her stepfather for eight years and that during that time he had never been kind to her. If she resisted when he wanted to have intercourse with her, he would beat her.

Helping the victim to sort out feelings toward the offender and other family members is an important step in treatment. In some cases, the child is angry at the mother for not protecting her from the father's sexual advances and may blame the mother even if she did not know what was taking place. The anger is accompanied by deep feelings of rejection if the child told the mother about the incest and she did nothing to stop it or did not believe the child's story. In either case, the child's trust in persons to whom she looked for affection and protection is shattered. A combination of group therapy and individual counseling enables the child to cope with feelings of distrust and begin to develop satisfying relationships with others.

Treating Adolescent Victims

Adolescent girls who have gone through an incestuous experience have confused and conflicting emotions after they have disclosed the incest to other family members. They are angry at their father who betrayed them, and they are angry at their mothers who failed to protect them. Some adolescent victims may believe that they are responsible for what happened because they did not stop the incest once it got underway. Others are depressed, use drugs or engage in various forms of self-destructive behavior. Therapists have discovered that many of these teenage girls have distorted perceptions about their bodies. They describe themselves as fat and ugly when they are actually very thin and quite attractive. These faulty perceptions and devaluations seem to be related to the low self-esteem and feelings of inadequacy that are commonly found in cases of father-daugher incest.

Group therapy has proven effective in helping adolescent female victims cope with these problems and with the anxieties that result from the incestuous experience. Linda Blick and Frances Porter, who have used the group approach at the Connecticut Sexual Trauma Treatment Program, observe that when they first enter the group many girls are passive and nonassertive.[1] They have also found that many adolescents manifest symptoms of depression and tend to withdraw from contact with their peers. As they begin to interact with other teenage girls who have gone through similar experiences, they are able to break through the isolation that has been associated with incest, begin to form friendships and are able to ventilate their emotional reactions in the supportive environment of the group.

Adolescent victims seek acceptance from their peers, and the group experience makes it possible for them to gain increased self-confidence when they receive praise and encouragement from group members. The distortion in body image begins to come under control so they no longer perceive themselves as unattractive, awkward or "damaged property." The therapists demonstrate the use of assertive techniques to help members who are shy and submissive to make decisions and act in their own best interests. Blick and Porter have found that building self-esteem is a slow and arduous process for these teenagers. "It can take months of continuous encouragement, reinforcement and praise before any significant behavioral changes are seen," they write. "These techniques are successful, however, if used consistently over time."

During group therapy, adolescents are encouraged to identify how they feel toward their fathers. Some members express fondness and affection and concede that the sexual relationship with their fathers or stepfathers had afforded them special attention, a sense of intimacy and power that was a payoff for sexual favors. Once the incest has been disclosed, the relationship between daughter and father is open to review. Group members are asked to decide what kind of relationship they want to have with their fathers. Some will decide to maintain a superficial relationship with him and others will decide to end all future contact. In some cases, the daughter will move toward trying to understand and accept her father's behavior. But in any case, the decision is regarded as the responsibility of the girls themselves rather than a choice that is made for them by others. Group therapists have found that adolescent victims are not inclined to talk openly about how they feel toward their mothers. They seem to refrain from expressing anger towards their mothers because by so doing their mothers would only reject them and turn away from them.

Group therapists introduce sex education as part of the group experience. Adolescent incest victims are tempted to engage in a series of sexual relationships to counteract the feeling that they are damaged by the incestuous experience. Therapy aims at preventing this form of acting out, destructive behavior and the consequences: unexpected pregnancy or sexually transmitted diseases. Lack of sound information about sexual functioning in many cases reinforces fears that some damage has been done during the sexual activity in which the daughter was involved. To clear up misunderstandings and answer questions, a physician meets with the group to supply accurate information and correct false ideas about sexual matters.

Group members who are waiting for a court hearing undergo considerable anxiety because they fear what will happen when they are called upon to testify. To help the girls prepare for the courtroom appearance, group members act out a simulated trial situation through role playing. Some members of the group have already gone through the court hearing and can explain what could happen in the event that the defense attorney becomes belligerent. Through the discussion and role playing, those who are facing the experience for the first time are able to testify creditably despite a highly charged situation when they appear as witnesses. Therapists also maintain contact with prosecutors, defense attorneys and judges in an effort to minimize the trauma that can result when the girl faces a hostile court that taxes her ability to function as a reliable witness.

Most adolescent incest victims are soon involved in the group process and look to the therapist and group members as important resources to help them deal with the impact of the sexual relationship with their fathers. But some girls are reluctant to participate and begin to talk about dropping out after they have participated in very few sessions. When the question of dropping out is raised, the therapist and group members point out that if the girl drops out of the group she risks further sexual abuse. Blick and Porter found that a number of girls who left the group did in fact undergo subsequent sexual abuse and returned to the group for help.

At various stages in the daughter's participation in the group sessions, her parents may object or question the value of the program. Parental opposition usually begins when the adolescent shows improved self-confidence and is more assertive in her relationship to family members. The victim's newfound self-confidence and personal growth can increase the intensity of parent-child conflict. Therapists anticipate the possibility that the parents will object to the daughter's involvement in the group program and discuss the matter with the parents early in the course of therapy. If the parents are aware that this problem may occur, the difficulty can usually be managed when it actually becomes an obstacle to the girl's continuing attendance at group meetings.

Helping Incest Victims' Mothers

The disclosure of an incestuous relation between the father and daughter has a significant impact on the mother. Although most mothers initially react by expressing concern for the child, this protective reaction may change when they consider their own self-interest. They are torn between protecting the child and protecting the husband. If the mother sides with the child, the husband may retaliate by physically attacking her in addition to withdrawing emotional and financial support. Under the strain, some mothers become immobilized and sink into a state of physical and emotional collapse.

Mothers often complain that they are fatigued. Clinicians point out that the fatigue usually masks depression in these mothers. They tend to be isolated, have few friends and lack the social skills that are needed to form relationships with others. They develop a passive-dependent personality in response to the dominance of their husband and maintain a chronic attitude of helplessness. Many cannot drive a car, handle money or manage a checking account. They may have difficulty coping with even the most trivial problems. It is not surprising, therefore, that many are ineffective in dealing with the incest problem. Some take immediate action to protect the daughter from further abuse, but many do not have the personal resources to take effective steps that will stop the incest from continuing. They are afraid of the responsibilities that fall upon them if they separate from their husbands and feel inadequate to deal with them.

Because of their personal and financial limitations, these

mothers require support and practical help in handling the impact of disclosure. Group therapy has proven to be an an effective way of helping them to function more adequately. The group experience also provides opportunities for mothers to develop social skills and break through the isolation that limits their relationships to persons within the family. Sgroi and Dana, who developed a special program for mothers of incest victims, outline the purposes of group therapy: (1) help mothers share their experience with others; (2) deal with unreasonable expectations about their husbands and men in general; (3) practice setting limits about relationships and family roles; (4) deal with anger in a constructive way; (5) break through the pattern of submissiveness; and (6) improve their social skills. Group members are also helped to deal with sexual issues. Many express anxiety and discomfort in talking with their daughters about menstruation, puberty and birth control. They also have problems in relating to their husbands in sexual intercourse, finding the experience unsatisfactory and regarding it as a routine that has to be tolerated but is not enjoyable. Because sexual adjustment problems are often related to the development of an incestuous relation, the objective is to improve the sexual relationship between the marital pair in the event the daughter is to remain in the home.

If the mother decides to separate from her husband or if he is imprisoned, mothers become totally responsible for handling financial matters. They can look to other group members who give direction in such matters as how to apply for public assistance and how to get support payments from their husbands in cases of divorce. The group also provides support to those mothers who are going through the criminal justice system. Group members explain the procedures involved and share their experiences. When combined with individual therapy, the group program is effective in helping mothers of daughters who are incest victims. Sgroi and Dana summarize their experience in the use of group therapy:

> As these mothers gathered support and strength from the group, they saw that they could be different and made attempts to gain control in their own lives and in their families. The increase in confidence and self-esteem begins as they take control of their own lives and assert themselves at home. We see the mother asserting her

rightful role in the family as being a clear indicator of success for
her, as well as an indicator of her heightened self-esteem.[2]

Most mothers of incest victims fail to establish limits between
themselves and their husbands, and between themselves and their
children. They permit their daughters to take over adult roles
within the family; blurring the generation lines then contributes
to the development of father-daughter incest. Mothers have difficulty accepting their part in incestuous behavior and tend to place
the entire blame on their husbands. In group therapy, mothers
who deny any responsibility for what has happened are challenged
by other group members who point out that mothers do share
blame by permitting the daughter to take over the mother role.
Mothers learn to establish boundaries and enforce limits on behavior as their sense of autonomy and assertiveness increases.
Group therapists use assertiveness training, role playing and role
modeling to help mothers achieve a greater sense of control within the family.

Many women in mother-therapy groups have no social network to support them. They usually have been socially isolated
and have no one in whom they can confide or turn to after the
incest has been disclosed. They feel that they cannot talk about
incest to their family or friends because most people are uncomfortable about intra-family sex. The group experience provides the
support they need to survive. Feelings of shame and guilt are no-
ticeably reduced when a mother connects with others who have
had the same experience. Sharing feelings in the supportive environment of the group with those who "have been in the same
boat," mothers are able to talk about their own childhoods, the
deprivation they suffered and their need for nurturing and affection. Some who were sexually abused by their fathers begin to
deal with their reactions to their own incestuous experiences for
the first time. Others talk about the physical abuse to which they
were subjected as children and their difficulty in establishing trusting relationships with others. The therapist reaches out with genuine friendliness and respect to help them form trusting relationships and respond to the supportive efforts of group members
without being afraid that they will be exploited or betrayed.

Treatment for Offenders

Because many cases of sexual abuse that come to the attention of law enforcement agencies involve father-daughter incest, special efforts are being made to understand the dynamics that underlie this form of sexual behavior. Professionals who have worked with these offenders find that they have deep-seated feelings of helplessness, vulnerability and dependency. When called upon to face a stressful situation or take adult responsibilities that are involved in marriage and parenthood, they feel highly inadequate and regress to a state of dependency and passivity. Groth points out that incest behavior is an attempt to compensate for personal inadequacies:

> Parent-child incest behavior is equivalent to symptom formation in that it serves to gratify a need, to defend against anxiety and to express unresolved conflict. The incestuous offender becomes dependent on sexual activity to meet his emotional needs. He finds adult sexual relationships which require negotiation, mutual reciprocity and shared commitment and investment either unsecurable or overtaxing and he turns to his child for sexual gratification of his needs without the demands of adult responsibility.[3]

The incestuous relationship serves several purposes for the offender. It validates his self-esteem, compensates for being rejected by his wife and restores a sense of power and control. Incest also gratifies a need for attention and affection, relieves loneliness and isolation and temporarily strengthens his sense of masculinity.

Dealing with Denial

When the incestuous father is confronted with the disclosure of incest, he frequently denies it. He may claim that his sexual offense was due to excessive drinking or he may allege that the victim was seductive and provoked him into the relationship. Professionals who have worked with incestuous fathers find that the offender's denials must be dealt with immediately if treatment is to succeed. The therapist must challenge the rationalizations that the offender puts forward to explain his behavior. If he insists that he was an innocent victim of the daughter's sexual manipulation, the therapist asks the father why he did not correct the daughter for her inappropriate behavior. Some fathers are not able to distinguish between normal behavior and seductive behavior. They misinterpret stylized feminine behavior as a sexual "come-on" when the daughter is not actually aware that she is creating a seductive image.

Therapists find that incest offenders have extreme difficulty admitting that the incest occurred or that they initiated the sexual behavior. Fear of being imprisoned, being separated from their families and the stigma involved sometimes lead the offender to give a fabricated account of how the incestuous relationship developed, as in the following case.

Al, a thirty-five-year-old blue-collar worker, was arrested for sexually molesting his twelve-year-old stepdaughter, Kathy. He admitted that he had an incestuous relationship with her and that it progressed to sexual intercourse. But Al steadfastly maintained that he did so only because Kathy insisted that he have sex with her. He told the probation officer that the stepdaughter threatened to tell her mother that he had raped her if he did not have intercourse with her. Al was referred for therapy on a court order.

During the initial stage of group therapy, Al continued to deny that he initiated the sexual activity with his stepdaughter. He described Kathy as a seductive and sexually precocious child who would "cling on any man that came along." Al pictured himself as the victim of her sexual aggressiveness, described in great detail how Kathy had encouraged him to fondle her breasts, and suggested that they engage in intercourse when her mother was away from home. Al told the group that "I am the one who was sexually abused. I didn't really abuse her. I'm just here to learn more about all this."

Al's persistent denial was challenged by other group members who did not accept his account of how the incest began. Eventually, he admitted that he had made up the story of how Kathy had seduced him. "It was the other way around," he explained. "I was just afraid to admit that I was the one who started the incest. I didn't want to go to jail. I normally tell the truth, but I didn't want to lose everything I had." Later, Al met with Kathy's therapist and in his stepdaughter's presence admitted that he was responsible for what had happened and apologized for the harm he had inflicted on her. "It was a big relief, like a weight was lifted off my chest, once I faced up to what I had really done," he concluded.

Some incest offenders make a qualified denial of their involvement with a daughter or stepdaughter. The following case illustrates how an incestuous father perceives the relationship as nonsexual and does not consider his behavior to constitute incest or sexual abuse.

Bob, a thirty-nine-year-old professional man, was referred for therapy by child-protection services when an investigation revealed that he had sexually molested his fourteen-year-old stepdaughter, Norma. Bob became involved in sexual contact with his stepdaughter during a weekend when his wife was away from home. He explained that he felt lonely and rejected by his wife and that Norma offered him the companionship that he needed. Bob did not want to become involved in an extramarital relationship because he considered adultery to be sinful. Moreover, he did not want to risk being rejected if he turned to someone other than his wife for emotional and sexual gratification. "I always had the fear of being rejected from my early childhood," he explained. "And I was being rejected by my wife. So with my stepdaughter it was different. I didn't have the fear of being rejected. So it was safer than going outside the family."

His stepdaughter, Norma, was someone with whom he could communicate and who was a source of comfort to him. When the relationship to Norma became sexualized, she felt uncomfortable, disclosed what had happened and was sent to live with her father. "In my mind, what I did wasn't sexual abuse," Bob told the therapist. "But in Norma's mind, I guess she thought of it as being that. When the welfare worker said it was sexual abuse, I was really surprised. I still thought it couldn't be that — that there was something really wrong with what I did." In group therapy, Bob was confronted about his sexual feelings toward his stepdaughter, and he denied that he had any strong sexual desires that led to the incest. Like many incest offenders, Bob denied that his behavior was motivated by a sexual attraction to his stepdaughter, and by viewing his behavior as devoid of any sexual desires, he could rationalize that he was not really commiting incest.

Fixated Offenders

Some incest offenders have a history of becoming sexually involved with prepubescent children rather than with adolescents. Fathers who become involved with younger children in the family are fixated at the childhood level of sexual and emotional maturation and have not achieved adult status in their sexual development. These fixated offenders have sometimes had a series of sexual contacts with both boys and girls, as illustrated in the following case study.

Carl, a forty-year-old man, was referred for therapy after having been involved in an incestuous relationship with his stepdaughter, Ruth, beginning when she was age seven and continuing for approximately five years. He had been married three times and had had many short-term sexual contacts with males beginning in early adolescence. All three marriages were highly unstable, and in each marriage, Carl became sexually involved with his wife's prepubescent children. None of the relationships with these stepdaughters progressed to sexual intercourse, but included exhibitionism, genital fondling and cunnilingus. The sexual activity with stepsons included masturbation and oral sex.

Carl's most extended incestuous relationship involved a stepdaughter, Ruth, whom he described as a very attractive, highly intelligent girl with whom he spent most of his time riding horseback, scubadiving and motorcycling. Ruth became Carl's constant companion, even assisted him in carrying on the small business operation that her stepfather operated. Carl began to lose interest in his wife as the relationship with his stepdaughter became more intimate. Ruth did not resist her stepfather's sexual advances. Eventually, she engaged in oral sex with him on a fairly regular basis. Carl romanticized the relationship to his stepdaughter to the point where he even had fantasies that one day she would marry him and that he would have a child by her.

Men with pedophilic tendencies do marry and have children, but they are inclined to feel emotionally immature and lonely in their marriages. Incestuous fathers who turn to latency-age chil-

the contact makes the man the child not the child a woman

dren in the family for sex are motivated by a desire to relive their childhood. As Carl explained, "When I was having sexual contacts with my stepdaughter I became more like a child; I felt like I was growing up with her. I guess that I was trying to relive my own childhood and that is what brought about the incest."

The sexual activity of these fixated incest offenders is limited to kissing, fondling, genital touching and oral sex contacts. They are usually nonviolent and threats are not used to get the child to cooperate in the sexual activity. In rare cases, the fixated offender may be an individual who is deeply disturbed. Therefore, a careful examination is made to determine if severe psychopathic traits or symptoms of psychosis are present. If the evaluation of the offender's personality indicates such disturbances, the offender is referred for inpatient therapy in a psychiatric facility.

Offenders in Group Therapy

Group therapy with incest offenders helps them learn to control their behavior and find appropriate outlets for sexual gratification. Treatment is directed toward enabling the incestuous father to: (1) recognize the unmet needs that underlie his behavior; (2) identify the stress factors that precipitate incest and learn how to avoid stress-producing situations; (3) develop constructive ways of dealing with stress; (4) detect early warning signals and interrupt the sequence of events that leads to incest. In order to achieve these goals the offender is seen in individual counseling sessions, in group therapy and in family therapy. In most cases, a combination of all three approaches is indicated.

Before entering group therapy, the offender is usually seen by a therapist who evaluates the individual's personality and assesses the nature of his behavior. Specific attention is focused on the social functioning of the offender and his capacity to recognize that his sexual abuse causes harm to others. The therapist also assesses the type of abuse involved, frequency and duration of the sexual activity and the relationship between the offender and the victim. The offender's defense mechanisms are studied to determine whether he uses denial, projection, rationalization, regression or minimization in trying to cope with the incest. Finally, the assessment results in conclusions as to the extent to which the offender is in control of his behavior and a judgment as to whether he is a dangerous person who has a weak ego and may resort to using force in sexual contacts and inflict pain on his victim.

The group process provides an opportunity for incest offenders to develop social skills, improve communication and change relationships with their spouses and children. Among the techniques used in group therapy are: role playing to show group members how their behavior appears to others; demonstration of relaxation exercises to help members cope with stress; and behavior rehearsal to teach members how to ask for positive strokes from their wives. Wives of offenders are invited to join the group, participate in exchanging ideas and explore their role in the incestuous triangle. In some cases, the group process is useful in helping the wife come to a decision as to whether she wants her husband to return to the family by examining the quality of the marital relationship. In most cases of father-daughter incest, sexual dissatisfaction is a contributing factor. The group therapist encourages members to explore their sexual attitudes and to understand how these attitudes grew out of their early-childhood experiences. Sex education is included to provide sound information about sexual anatomy, sexual feelings and the range of outlets available to meet erotic needs.

Group members are also encouraged to find sources of personal fulfillment that will bolster self-esteem and thereby avoid destructive patterns of defense such as heavy drinking or suicidal attempts. Group support is especially important if incest results in divorce, because the offender will undergo a fairly prolonged period of stress and depression when he is separated from his family. The emotional support and understanding provided by other group members will help the offender survive the separation and rebuild his life.

Parents In Group Therapy

Some communities have developed programs of group therapy for the parents of incestuous families with the purpose of bringing about changes in the marital relationship that can prevent the recurrence of incest. Blair and Rita Justice have employed this approach in working with couples at Houston, Texas and find that it is an effective method for solving problems related to incest.[4] When a new couple enters the group, they are asked to fill out a checklist of problems and rank them in order of their importance. The typical couple identifies problems in one or more of these six areas: symbiosis, marital relationships, stress reduction, sexual climate, isolation or alcoholism. Once the checklist has been completed and the problems have been clearly identified, the couple sets out the goals that they want to achieve during the course of therapy. The goals are expressed in terms of behavior changes that are to take place during the next three months. For example, if the couple identifies isolation as a problem, the agreement would be that they will go out with friends once per week. Or if alcoholism is a problem to be worked on during therapy, the contract might specify that total abstinence will be achieved by the end of three months.

In most cases, the objective of group therapy is to break up the excessive dependency between the husband and wife so each partner can become autonomous and self-sufficient. To improve the marital relationship, the couple is taught to relate to each other in positive ways by asking for positive strokes, expressing feelings of affection and responding to requests for emotional support. Group members are encouraged to discuss their sexual difficulties and make agreements that will bring about a more satisfying experience for both partners. As the sex relationship improves, the need to turn to a child for sexual gratification is eliminated and the generation boundaries between parent and child are strengthened.

The group process also provides an opportunity for the couple to form ties with other group members and break the pattern of social isolation that often accompanies incest. Parents are required to make new friends and to engage in social activities that will broaden their contacts outside the family and yield a sense of personal fulfillment. Because stress is an important factor in creating incest, couples are taught to manage stress by using relaxation exercises to reduce tension and avoid excessive fatigue. The sexual climate of the home is also examined, including the sexual attitudes of both marital partners. Parents are taught the differences between nonsexual forms of affection and sexually stimulating behavior and learn how to avoid erotic contact with their children. Alcoholism is a problem for many couples who come into group therapy. In these cases, the couple is encouraged to participate in Alcoholics Anonymous because of the structure and reinforcement that AA provides to help members stop drinking.

A similar parent-group-therapy program has been in operation in Santa Clara, California under the direction of Henry Giaretto, who has developed a humanistic approach to the treatment of father-daughter incest.[5] The group program emphasizes social responsibiltiy and the possibility of personal growth as a basis for individual and family living. The therapist draws on various techniques that enable group members to develop a strong sense of self-identification and gain control of their lives. Gestalt therapy, conjoint therapy, psychodrama, transactional analysis and personal journals are used to accomplish these therapeutic ends. The major objectives of the program, referred to as the Child Sexual Abuse Treatment Program (CSATP), include these:

1. Provide immediate counseling and practical assistance to sexually abused children and their families, in particular to victims of father-daughter incest.
2. Hasten the process of reconstitution of the family and of the marriage, if possible, since children prosper best in normally functioning families headed by natural parents.
3. Marshall and coordinate all official services responsible to the sexually abused child and family, as well as private resources to ensure comprehensive case management.
4. Employ a treatment model that fosters self-managed growth of individuals capable of positive contributions to society, rather than a medical model based on the vagaries of mental disease.

The group therapy program for parents is called Parents United and is based on the premise that the marital relationship is a key factor in the development of father-daughter incest, that incestuous behavior is not likely to occur if parents enjoy mutually beneficial relations and if each partner has a high self-concept. "Individuals with high self-concepts are not apt to engage others in hostile-aggressive behavior," writes Giarretto. "In particular, they do not undermine the self-concept of their mates or children through incestuous behavior. Individuals who have low self-concepts are usually angry, disillusioned, and feel they have little to lose. They are thus primed for behavior that is destructive to others and to themselves." The program assumes that everyone can learn to control the way he behaves and ultimately the course his life will take. Group members are encouraged to identify weaknesses and habits that need to be eliminated such as the uncontrolled use of drugs, food or alcohol. The concept of self-management is introduced as an essential in the development of a high self-concept. Each group member is helped to realize his potential and achieve a higher level of personal fulfillment. Once this goal has been achieved, the need to turn to another family member for a sense of identity will be eliminated and the possibility of incest will have been reduced.

The results of the Parents United Program initiated by Giarretto are encouraging. In 90 percent of the families who were referred to CSATP, the children were returned to their families within the first month and about 90 percent of the marriages have been saved. Previous to CSATP, individual or marriage counseling occurred only after release from jail, if at all. Under the new approach, the offender's rehabilitation starts soon after his arrest and the difficult task of establishing a normal nonincestuous relationship between father and daughter is accomplished in much less time. Offenders who would have received long prison terms are given suspended sentences or placed on probation as an alternative to incarceration.

Parents United is rapidly expanding as a resource for the treatment of incest and shows promise of developing into a model for other communities. As of March 1979, CSATP had provided services for more than two thousand families, and eighteen new programs with chapters of Parents United have been started in other California cities. The success of Parents United is due to the principle on which it is based, namely, that the needs of the entire family — parents as well as children — must be considered in the treatment of incest.

Helping Victims as Adults

The consequences of incest are far reaching and affect the

lives of thousands of victims in their adult years. Most victims keep the incest secret hidden from others for as long as twenty or thirty years and have never discussed the experience with others who have undergone a similar situation as children or adolescents. The stigma that is attached to incest is a formidable obstacle to sharing feelings or talking about the problems that incest victims face. But gradually the barriers that surround incest are beginning to be overcome. Woman victims are now recognizing that the secrecy makes it possible for incestuous behavior to continue without interference, and they are beginning to talk and write about the effects of incest on the victims and their families.

To help women who have been victimized deal with these aftereffects, some communities have initiated programs of individual and group therapy for adult incest victims. One such program has been developed by the Child Guidance and Evaluation Center at Austin, Texas. Recognizing the need for a special service for adult incest victims, Jan MacLean — a social worker on the center's staff — announced that a meeting for incest victims would be called to explore the possibility of forming a support group. The first meeting was attended by three former incest victims. Within a few weeks, the group had grown to accommodate ten members and plans for further expansion of the service got underway. The weekly group meetings provide an opportunity for the members to discuss their mutual problems and to express their feelings about what happened to them as children and teenagers. One member was sexually abused by her brother at the age of three. Another was assaulted by her uncle at a very young age. One past victim was sexually abused by her grandfather, her uncle, a cousin, and her father. Other group members had been involved in father-daughter incest during puberty and adolescence.

Some group members have been in psychotherapy or individual counseling. They reported that the therapist to whom they turned for help did not really want to discuss the incest experience but directed attention to other matters during the course of therapy. Some victims were reluctant to reveal the source of their anxiety and depression to the therapist. One woman describes her experience.

This is all part of a long story that I've never fully told anyone, not even my psychiatrist. I like him and I want to talk to him, but I guess I'm afraid of him, too. I want to fall in love someday and get married and have children. But I'm afraid. I am afraid of men, and I'm afraid to be touched. I want to be able to touch people and to be touched, but I just can't bear it. I feel guilty about everything and feel like somehow it must have all been my fault.

The group experience provides a secure environment in which past incest victims can discuss their feelings of guilt and help each other come to better terms with themselves. Most of the women in the group have been struggling with depression and low self-esteem for years and are trying to regain a measure of self-worth and rebuild their lives. The group interaction is a source of renewed energy for the members. They are enabled to mobilize their personal resources through the encouragement they receive from other group members. Many have had a new start. Some have become settled in professional careers as teachers and child-care workers. Others are trying to work out a satisfactory relationship to marital partners. All are benefiting by the strong support and understanding that the group experience provides.

Family Therapy

Social workers and mental health professionals also use family therapy to solve problems that directly or indirectly relate to the development and maintenance of incest. The family therapy approach to incest is based on the premise that the family is an organic system and that family members behave in ways that keep the system in balance. When the balance of the family is disturbed in some way, various symptoms begin to appear. These symptoms indicate that the family is in trouble. Family therapists hold that incest is one symptom of a disturbance in family functioning. Therefore, the treatment of incest involves active intervention to bring about changes within the family system itself as well as within the individual family members.

Family therapy moves through several stages. In the initial phase, the therapist generates a warm and optimistic atmosphere so that family members can talk openly about the anger, hurt and shame that often accompany the disclosure of the incestuous relationship. Once the family members express their reactions to the disclosure, the therapist assures them that their situation is not as hopeless as they might believe and that they can move on with their lives despite the pain and disillusionment they are undergoing. The therapist then suggests that each family member can help in reuniting the family on a firm basis and that solving the problems that beset the family will require the help of everyone.

Assessing Family Functioning

Assessing family functioning is an important initial step in helping incestuous families. The assessment of the family system includes a careful evaluation of family structure and of communication and negotiation of conflicts. In examining the family structure, the therapist attempts to find answers to the following questions:

1. How are the roles of husband and wife defined?
2. How well do parents carry out their parental roles within the family?
3. How is power distributed among family members?
4. What are the alignments and splits between family members?
5. In what areas is power shared?
6. How are autonomy and independence encouraged?
7. How well are generational boundaries defined and maintained?

An assessment of the communication processes and patterns of interaction among family members includes an exploration of the following matters:

1. How well does the family system allow opportunities for open and honest communication?
2. What limitations are placed on expression of feelings?
3. In what form are messages transmitted?
4. How is communication used in resolving problems?
5. What are the major obstacles to effective communication?

The assessment involves a study of how the family negotiates conflict and differences among family members and raises the following questions:

1. What is the family's typical approach to solving problems?
2. In what areas does negotiation succeed or fail?
3. Who initiates the negotiation process?
4. Does the family have a varied and flexible approach to solving problems?
5. What mechanisms are used to cope with crisis situations?

A careful examination of these areas of family functioning results in the development of a treatment plan that will improve family relationships, open channels of communication and enable the family to cope with conflict and stress. The use of this approach to working with incestuous families is illustrated in the following case study.

The Whitcomb Family

Joe Whitcomb, a forty-five-year-old postal worker, is the father of three children. He became involved in an incestuous relationship with his oldest daughter, Leslie, when she was age fourteen. In most respects, Joe's life had been quite normal, but when he reached his fortieth birthday, he began to have episodes of mild depression during which he withdrew from his family for a day or two at a time. Joe's wife, Rose, would try to inquire into why Joe was unhappy. His response was always the same: "I don't really know. I'll just have to tough it out and wait till things look a little brighter." Because the moods dissipated in a few days, neither Joe or his wife thought professional help was needed to enable him to cope with his moodiness.

Joe's job did not pay very well and growing children brought increased expenses. Bills went unpaid, the financial problems increased and Joe began to feel helpless and inadequate. To ease the strain, Rose decided to apply for work in one of the local department stores. She was employed as a sales clerk three days each week. Her employer asked her to work until nine o'clock in the evening. In order to do this, Rose asked Leslie to take over some of the household chores such as preparing the evening meals, putting her younger brother and sister to bed and cleaning up after the children. Leslie was thirteen at that time. She was developing into a very attractive adolescent and reminded Joe of his wife when he first met her. Leslie's father remarked about how mature she appeared and expressed appreciation for the way she took over many of the household duties.

When Rose worked late in the evening, Joe would begin to drink just to relax. After the dinner dishes had been cleared and the younger children had been put to bed, Leslie would join her father in the living room to watch television or to engage in conversation. The relationship between Leslie and her father became rather close and intimate. Joe would tell Leslie how lonely he felt, especially now that Rose was gone in the evenings. He hinted that he was not happy in the marriage, that things were not going well and that his wife rejected him. Leslie filled a void in Joe's life and he began to look to her more and more for companionship. The quiet evenings with her father were also a source of enjoyment for Leslie because she felt that her father loved and admired her. Her father rewarded her with small gifts and gave her special privileges. Meanwhile, Leslie's relationship with her mother began to deteriorate. She complained that her mother never had time to listen to her problems and was more interested in her job than in the family.

One evening, Leslie was talking to her father and confiding her feelings about her mother. Joe put his arm around her and she fell asleep. As she rested her head against his shoulder, Joe had a feeling of being sexually aroused. For the first time, he realized that his relationship with his daughter had become erotically stimulating, but he pushed any thoughts of having sexual contacts with her out of his mind. Yet, the temptation to seduce her was always there. Leslie's sexual development made her very attractive and kept Joe aware of his need for affection and sexual gratification. Gradually, Joe began to seek out opportunities to touch Leslie's breasts when she came near him. Eventually, he began to teach her how to excite him by stroking his penis while he masturbated her.

Rose discovered the sexual relationship between Joe and Leslie when she came home early from work one evening. An intense confrontation followed. Rose said that she could never trust either of them again and that the "whole thing is utterly disgusting." Joe was humiliated, and Leslie was ashamed of what had happened. Rose threatened to divorce Joe and never permit him to see the children again. Joe voluntarily moved out of the home to relieve the tension that followed after the incest had been discovered. Rose considered filing criminal charges against her husband, but the district attorney suggested that she consult with a social worker who could evaluate the family situation before legal action was taken.

The social worker talked with Rose and suggested that counseling might be an alternative to divorce or criminal action. Rose decided to accept the social worker's offer to counsel her in order to help her arrive at a decision. After three weeks, Rose decided that she did not want to divorce her husband. She recognized that in the past he had been a responsible husband and father. She told the social worker that she recognized that there were serious marital problems before the incest developed and that she and her husband needed professional help to resolve them. Meanwhile, Joe consulted a therapist who worked with sex offenders. At first, Joe avoided talking about his part in initiating the incestuous relationship with Leslie. The therapist pointed out that he could not escape responsibility for his behavior and would have to admit to his wife and daughter that he was to blame for what happened. Eventually, Joe accepted total responsibility for the incest and admitted to his wife and daughter that he should not have let his behavior get out of control. He assured Leslie that she was not to blame and told her that he was genuinely sorry for what had happened. Joe expressed the hope that a suitable plan could be worked out for him to rejoin his family and promised that the incestuous behavior would not be repeated. Joe's wife was not prepared to make a definite decision. She said she might be willing to give it a try, but that she could not forgive her husband for what happened.

Eventually Joe and Rose agreed to meet with the therapist for a series of family therapy sessions and explore how they felt about their marriage. These family therapy sessions were also designed to give the parents an opportunity to exchange feelings about the incest and how it developed over a period of several months. The first session was devoted to each partner's reaction to the disclosure. Rose said that she did not think she could overcome the feelings of anger and distrust because of what happened when she was gone from home. Joe recognized that it would be difficult for his wife to trust him. "I know it was wrong, and I know that I am responsible for it and I can't blame you for feeling angry about it," said Joe.

In the second family therapy session, the couple began to consider what steps could be taken to avoid the possibility that incest might happen again. Rose said that the only way she could feel secure would be to require that Joe not be left alone with the children. Joe suggested that he could take a second job working part time in the evening and on weekends. Then Rose could quit her job and stay at home to care for the children. "I'd like to get into something different anyway," Joe told Rose. "When I was in high school, I took up auto mechanics. I never had a chance to use what I learned. I'm rusty, of course, but I think I could pick it up again. At least I'd like to try. It pays well and I'd be doing something I really like. That's part of the problem. My job bores the hell out of me. If I had something interesting to do — to look forward to and plan for — I think things would fall into place."

Rose listened to Joe's proposal in complete astonishment. "I had no idea you weren't happy working at the post office," she said. "I know you were moody at times, but you never told me what was on your mind. How was I to know what was wrong? Sometimes I thought maybe I had said something you didn't like or upset you in some way. You always keep things to yourself."

Joe took an important step forward by telling his wife about his frustrations and sharing his ideas with her. The therapist asked him why he had not done this before. "I guess I thought she really didn't want to hear about my problems. She had enough of her own. So I just sort of kept on feeling sorry for myself and telling myself there was no point in trying to explain how I felt."

"I'd like to know if something is bothering you," Rose said. "It's not knowing that is hard on me. And I can't know unless you tell me and help me understand."

The therapist assured Joe that it was going to be difficult for him to change his accustomed way of dealing with his feelings, but that it was important for him to try. The third family therapy session was a breakthrough in overcoming communication obstacles. Joe said that he had never told Rose how much he really loved her. "I guess it is because I didn't think you really loved me. Maybe that you just put up with me, but that I didn't really mean all that much to you. And I felt we were kind of drifting apart. Anyway, something has been missing. I'm not sure what. And I don't know if we can do anything about it now."

Rose reached out to touch Joe. "I know. I'm missing something too. I want to feel close to you. I feel closer now. Maybe we can do something about it. I know that I haven't been very loving either. And yet I know it is important to you. It's just that sometimes making love − I mean I know that sometimes I don't respond. Not the way I would like to, when we are making love. And that must be a disappointment for you."

The therapist pointed out that sexual dissatisfaction often leads to feelings of rejection and causes serious problems between husbands and wives. He also assured the couple that the sexual adjustment could be improved if they both wanted to make the effort. He pointed out that they had already made a good beginning by talking about the sexual relationship and suggested that the next two sessions be used to help them explore their mutual needs and develop a better understanding of how they could achieve satisfaction in their sexual relationship. Leslie was not included in these sessions but was invited to participate in a subsequent discussion of problems that related more directly to her. This session provided an opportunity for Leslie to express her feelings of alienation from her mother and the guilt associated with the incestuous experience. The parents both helped clear up some misunderstandings about Leslie's part in what happened and made her aware of what caused her father to turn to her for emotional and sexual gratification. The therapist pointed out that it was important for the parents to help Leslie assume a normal child role in the family rather than assuming an adult role. The mother explained that she had allowed and expected her daughter to take over too much responsibility for taking care of the family, but that in the future this would be changed. Leslie was concerned that her father "might try it again." The parents explained that in the future close, personal contacts between her and her father would be avoided and that the mother would always be there to protect Leslie if anything occurred that might lead to a continuation of the father's incestuous behavior.

After six months of therapy, the family decided to reunite. They continued in therapy for another six months after the father returned home and there has been no repetition of incest.

Working with Involuntary Clients

Most families, unlike the Whitcombs, do not seek help voluntarily because they are reluctant to admit that they have a problem and are sensitive to the stigma that attaches to intra-familial sex. These families will not engage in family or group therapy unless an outside source requires them to do so. Therefore, professional persons who work with incestuous families recognize that they will be dealing with resistive clients and that unconventional approaches are needed to get these involuntary clients to participate in therapy. The therapist uses the authority of law enforcement agencies to keep the family involved in therapy and also uses the authority inherent in his or her position as a professional person by insisting that sexually abusive behavior is not acceptable and must stop. Most families need to feel the personal authority of the therapist and the authority of law if they are to be helped.

Therapists also use aggressive outreach in working with involuntary clients, take extraordinary measures to help the family come to therapy sessions, provide transportation to and from the treatment center and assign buddies to family members. Sgroi points out that aggressive outreach requires hard work and long hours in addition to professional skill. "Since involuntary clients will not, as a rule, 'come' to treatment, helping strategies must be characterized by an aggressive outreach," she writes. "It will be necessary to pursue these clients with something that 'feels like help'. They will present initially with hostility, fear, isolation, avoidance and denial. Treatment programs must be willing to go after these clients."[6]

Many of the involuntary clients also face a wide variety of problems that requires the therapist to provide concrete services in addition to the usual intervention methods. If the family is having severe difficulty functioning in a number of areas, a program of total life support is offered in order to help them survive the impact of disclosure. If the father is removed from the home, the family undergoes a period of unusual stress, including social and economic upheaval and deprivation. In some cases, they lack basic necessities such as food, clothing and money. In other cases, the therapist provides guidance and encouragement to enable the family to use its own personal resources to survive. In each case, the treatment plan is based on a careful consideration of which problems need attention and which forms of intervention will be most effective in bringing about a resolution of the difficulties the family must face.

Intervention usually proceeds through several phases. Individual therapy with the victim begins as soon as possible and continues until there is enough time for the initial trauma to subside. Group therapy is the preferred treatment for adolescents, after individual therapy has provided enough strength for entering into the group. Because the experience is painful for mothers, they are included in a group-therapy program where they can receive peer support. Special therapeutic measures for the incestuous father should also be available to help him correct and control his immature sexual behavior. Family therapy is effective if the parents are honestly willing and ready to take total responsibility for the sexual abuse and if they can provide adequate protection for the incest victim. Experience indicates that no one approach is effective in the treatment of incest. Intervention that includes individual and group therapy for victims and integrates them with therapy for the entire family points the way toward an intelligent and humane approach to helping incest victims and their families.

REFERENCES

1. Blick, L., and Porter, F.: Group therapy with adolescent female incest victims. In Sgroi, S.: *Handbook of Clinical Intervention in Child Sexual Abuse.* Lexington, Mass., Lexington Books, 1982, pp. 147-176.
2. Sgroi, S., and Dana, N.: Individual and group treatment of mothers of incest victims. In Sgroi, S.: *Handbook of Clinical Intervention in Child Sexual Abuse,* pp. 191-214.
3. Groth, N.: The incest offender. In Sgroi, S.: *Handbook of Clinical Inter-*

vention in Child Sexual Abuse, p. 227.

4. Justice, B., and Justice, R.: *The Broken Taboo.* New York, Human Sciences, 1979, pp. 242-252.

5. Giarretto, H.: Humanistic treatment of father-daughter incest. In Schultz L. (Ed.): *The Sexual Victimology of Youth.* Thomas, Springfield, 1980, pp. 140-163.

6. Sgroi, S.: Family treatment. In Sgroi, S., *Handbook of Clinical Intervention in Child Sexual Abuse,* p. 260.

Chapter 5

USING THE LEGAL SYSTEM

All I could do was picture my
father in prison for years to
come, without the kids, without nobody. All I could do
was visualize him sitting in
a cell, just thinking. That
hurt.

An incest victim

ALL states have passed laws forbidding incest. But the legal
definition of what constitutes incest varies. In most states,
only sexual intercourse between blood-related persons is regarded
as incest. Twenty-four states have broadened the definition to include sexual intercourse between stepparents and stepchildren.
Only five states regard all forms of sexual contact between family
members as coming within the legal definition of incest. Many
state statutes distinguish between sexual intercourse and other
forms of sexual interaction such as masturbation, exhibitionism
and oral-genital contact between family members. In these states,
behavior that does not include intercourse is designated as "carnal abuse of a child," "corrupting the morals of a minor," or "taking indecent liberties with a child." These forms of sexual behavior are regarded as less serious offenses than incest that involves
sexual intercourse between related persons.

Sexual intercourse is dealt with more severely than other
forms of sexual contact in most states. In Alaska, if the behavior
includes penetration of a child under the age of thirteen, the offender faces twenty years in prison. However, if the sexual contact

between the adult family member and the child does not include penetration, the maximum sentence is only five years. The severity of the penalty also varies with the age of the child who is the victim of sexual assault. In Mississippi, the law provides for life imprisonment or death in cases of carnal knowledge of a child under the age of twelve. If the victim is over twelve and under eighteen, the penalty is reduced to a fine of five hundred dollars, six months in the county jail or up to five years in prison. In seventeen states, a father could receive a life sentence for engaging in sexual intercourse with a preadolescent daughter. In three states, Florida, Mississippi and Oklahoma, he might even receive the death penalty.

However, very few of those charged with sexual offenses are brought to trial in cases involving family members. The Child Advocate Association of Chicago estimates that only 12 percent of intra-family sexual abuse is reported to the police. Another study of sex offenses against female children indicated that only 6 percent of over 300 women who had sexual experiences with adults before the age of thirteen reported the incident to the police. The obstacles to prosecution of the father who sexually abuses his daughter are numerous. The victim often endures the abuse rather than subject the father to the risk of being imprisoned or separated from the family. Some victims also fear that their fathers will take revenge if the facts are revealed to the police or other authorities. Herman points out that "no matter how miserable a daughter may be, she is likely to remain silent as long as she fears that a word from her will loose the full vengeance of the law upon her father, her family and herself."[1]

If a complaint is filed against the father, the probability that he will be brought to trial for incest is slight. A study of 250 reports of child sexual abuse in New York City showed that only 25 percent of those accused were ever brought to trial. The remaining cases were dismissed because no corroborating evidence was available, because the prosecutor thought the child would not make a credible witness or because the family wanted to spare the child from the rigors of the court experience. Thirty-eight of the men charged with an offense involving sexual abuse of children pleaded guilty to lesser charges. Fifteen went to trial and were found guilty. Over half of those convicted received fines or suspended sentences. Only 9 percent were sentenced to prison terms, most of them for a period of one year or less.[2]

Commenting on this study, Rush points out that there is a reluctance on the part of the legal system to prosecute sex offenders. "Because of a general reluctance to establish the sexual abuse of children as a serious offense and a tendency to forgive the molester and blame the victim," writes Rush, "the law and its agencies have made prosecution of sexual offenses against children so difficult that they are almost never apprehended, convicted, sentenced or imprisoned."[3]

Investigating Incest Charges

When criminal charges are brought against the father, the child and the family become involved in a process that is drawn-out and emotionally exhausting. Law enforcement officials question the victim in great detail to determine if the complaint can be substantiated. Medical personnel make a thorough examination to corroborate the victim's account of what happened. Once these preliminary steps are completed, the prosecutor determines if sufficient evidence exists to bring the case to trial. He interviews the victim and reviews the information gathered by law enforcement officers and protective service workers assigned to investigate the case. Eventually, the court process begins. The child is often required to testify in open court before a jury. Prosecutors usually prepare the child for what will take place during the trial, but the actual experience is often trying and emotionally exhausting for the incest victim and the family.

Most investigation of sexual abuse involves gathering information from the child victim. Sometimes a police officer who has been trained to conduct such interviews is available. In most states, a social worker on the staff of a child-protection agency is responsible for interviewing the child. The child is questioned about when the incestuous relationship began, the sexual behavior involved and the reaction of the victim to the incestuous experience. To carry out this important and sensitive task, the interviewer establishes a trusting relationship with the child by explaining the purpose of the interview at the outset. The child's co-

operation can usually be obtained if the interviewer explains the
reasons for asking when and how the incest began. Interviewers
may make statements that are reassuring to the victim, such as:
"I talk with many children who have had something like this
happen to them." The interviewer also may assure the child that
supplying information will give protection from further sexual
abuse. The interviewer avoids technical jargon because technical
terms tend to confuse the child and increase the victim's anxiety.
As the child begins to relax, the picture of what has occurred will
usually emerge spontaneously.

Very young children have limited verbal skills, and interviewers often use dolls and other media to help them reveal that actually happened to them. The Sexual Trauma Treatment Program
at Hartford, Connecticut has pioneered the use of art therapy to di-
agnose and treat sexually abused children. An art therapist works
with the other staff members, employing a wide range of materials such as clay, paints, chalk and other media. Children are
permitted to select the materials they prefer to express their feelings and describe their problems. Clara Stember, an art therapist
who worked in the program, reports that this approach provides
information that could not otherwise be obtained. "Art expression
is a nonthreatening approach," she writes. "For deeply hurt
people, protection of feeling is often necessary. By accepting
this fact, the art therapist can help others see feelings in drawings without otherwise demanding that the patient reveal the
hurt. In this way, the artwork acts as a vehicle for pulling together feelings and expression."[4]

Stember uses the "Winnicott Squiggle" game to obtain information that can be used in assessing the nature of the abuse and
the child's reactions to it. The game begins by asking the child
to choose a drawing instrument, usually a pencil or piece of cra-
yon. The therapist then tells the child: "I'm going to close my
eyes and make a little squiggle on this piece of paper. Then you
can make it into a picture." Next, the therapist joins in the game
by asking the child to make the squiggle. This process gives the
child an opportunity to participate in an exchange with the therapist, and the drawings are used to determine the nature of the
child's anxiety. "The inner turmoil and conflict of many sexually

abused children is directly responsive to art therapy," Stember reports. "Not only is art healing in itself, but since the sexual trauma is usually primarily psychological, artwork can provide a vehicle for bringing deeply repressed trauma to the surface."[5]

If the parents are in collusion to prevent the child from being contacted by authorities, obtaining access to the child may be impeded. Or, if the victim has confided in someone outside the family such as a teacher, day-care worker or health professional, these persons are reluctant to give authorities permission to talk with the child. Moreover, school officials may be unwilling to permit law enforcement or protective service workers to interview the child without first obtaining the parents' consent. Likewise, hospital and health officials are reluctant to undertake a physical examination of the victim unless the parent has given consent. If it is not possible to gain consent from the parents, a petition asking for temporary custody of the child can be filed, and the state can give consent for examination and treatment. As yet, few states have enacted laws that give minors the right to consent to a comprehensive examination without prior parental permission in cases of sexual assault. The passage of such legislation would avoid the obstacles that are now encountered in investigating incest complaints.

Building a valid case often depends on the child's testimony. Sometimes the information given by the child is the only basis for filing a charge against the perpetrator. Therefore, the child victim may be questioned by a law enforcement official, a detective or a prosecutor, in addition to the social worker or doctor. The redundant questioning procedure is often unproductive because the child has a limited capacity to undergo repeated questioning, and children tend to become confused in the process of investigation. Therefore, some jurisdictions have developed a coordinated approach in working with the incest victim. To avoid unnecessary and anxiety-provoking duplication in interviewing, all those who are interested in interviewing the the child participate in questioning the victim, and one person is designated to take a statement that can be used in the trial. The use of videotape recordings of the interview with the child has been instituted in some jurisdictions. The prosecutor views the videotaped recording to determine if the child is a capable witness without having to question the child independently.

The outcome of legal procedures in the prosecution of sex offenders often depends on the reliability of the child's testimony. Do children fantasize that incest has occurred? Do they exaggerate and give false or misleading information? Those who have worked with child victims think not. Henry Giarretto of the Child Abuse Program in San Jose estimates that less than 1 percent of the reports received by the center proved to be false.[6] In Albuquerque, New Mexico, a child-protective agency found that of the forty-six families in which complaints were made, only one allegation of incest proved to be unfounded. Kenneth Carpenter, director of the Special Services Division for the Department of Justice, states that children seldom fabricate stories of sexual abuse: "There is no evidence in the literature or among the service providers that children are unable to distinguish fact from fantasy in these situations. Of course, the younger the child, the more unlikely it is that the child would, or even could, imagine such things in the detail and accuracy with which children report these incidents."[7] Criminologist Fred Inbau and his colleague John Reid found that rarely do children falsify a sex-abuse report. In fact, the overwhelming majority of females who have been subjected to some form of sexual assault or abuse are reluctant to reveal the details of the sexual activity to which they have been subjected.

In some cases, the child victim is intimidated into denying that incest has occurred when confronted with the complicated process of stating what happened, being questioned repeatedly and subjected to intense cross-examination. A young victim gave this account of her experience:

She was first molested by her father before she entered kindergarten. The relationship continued in secret, but eventually she told her grade-school teacher what was happening. To avoid a scandal in the small town in which the family lived, the father agreed to undertake therapy and the incident was kept out of the local newspaper. However, the sexual abuse did not cease. When she was age eleven, her father raped her. The rape led to a divorce, and Judy went to live with her mother. A few months later, the mother's boyfriend began to make sexual advances. Judy attempted to escape his sexual molestation, but the sexual advances continued. She then went to the police asking for protection and insisted that her mother not be told about the complaint. The police promised that they would take steps to protect her from the mother's boyfriend.

"Noting happened for awhile after that," Judy recalled. "Then one day all my worst fears came true. Two policemen came to the door of my school classroom and said I had to come with them. When we got to the police station, my mother and Bob, her boyfriend, were there. They were both in handcuffs. They were sent to jail and I went to a juvenile home. It was terrible there: peanut butter and jelly sandwiches for dinner and a lot of tough street kids who were a lot different from me. I felt terrible and I was scared most of the time. All I wanted was to be home and be with my mother. I felt so rotten and ashamed for getting her into trouble. When she was released from jail, she tried to see me, but I felt so guilty for what I had done to her that I couldn't bear it."

Soon after Judy was admitted to the detention center, her mother asked a lawyer to visit her. The attorney talked with Judy about the upcoming trial. "He explained to me that the only way I'd ever get home and be with my mother would be to lie and say that I had made up the whole thing," Judy recalled. "If I didn't do that, he said they would lock me up forever. I didn't want to lie, but I wanted to go home so bad that it was all I could think about." A few days later, Judy's mother and the lawyer visited Judy at the detention center and coached her about what she should tell the court. Judy was to testify that she had made up the story about the sexual abuse because she had asked her mother's boyfriend to buy her a new dress and he had refused. So she had decided to get him into trouble by accusing him of sexual intimacy. The lawyer rehearsed her in how she was to testify. "We went over and over it," Judy said, "When we got to court, I told the lie just as we had rehearsed it."

"As soon as I said it," Judy continued, "everybody in the courtroom went crazy. Everyone was talking at once and shouting. There was a lot of talk about illegally gathering evidence, about me and what I'd done and about a place called Clairmont. When it finally got through to me that they were going to send me there, I kept saying, 'But what is this place called Clairmont?' I thought I was going to go home. I didn't know anything about commitment to psychiatric hospitals. I only knew that they were sending me away. And I remember my mother explaining to me that it was only for sixty days — that it was better for me to go to that place then for her to go to jail for years.''

After Judy entered the hospital, she was questioned about her testimony by the hospital staff. "By that time, I had built the lie into a forty-five minute story," Judy said. "Even I hardly knew what was true and what wasn't anymore. I felt crazy." Suspecting that Judy had given a false account of what happened, the doctor threatened to inject her with "truth serum" in order to get at the truth. Judy then decided to tell the truth in the hope that she would be released and could return to live with her mother. However, such was not the case. At the age of fourteen, she was transferred from the psychiatric hospital to a school for delinquent and emotionally disturbed girls.

The Medical Examination

In most jurisdictions, a medical examination is required in cases where sexual abuse is suspected. The findings of the medical examiner are reported to police or protective service agencies and become part of the evidence that is used in prosecuting the offender. The reports are then used to corroborate the child's story if there is evidence that sexual abuse did occur according to the medical findings. The National Center for Child Abuse recommends that all suspected cases of incest receive immediate attention from a qualified pediatrician, who is sensitive to the emotional trauma involved in sexual abuse and who can give attention to the psychological and emotional aspects of the patient during the course of the examination. The examination is carried on in a relaxed manner with sufficient time to obtain a detailed history from the patient. If the physician does not have enough time to get this information, a clinical social worker is called upon to talk with the victim.

The medical examination includes a complete medical history

of the patient and identification of all trauma, with special emphasis on genital, oral and rectal injury. A careful description of the genital anatomy is included regardless of whether trauma is present. Tests for the presence of sperm in female children and tests for venereal disease, including a blood test for syphilis, are included as part of the examination. Documentation of the presence of any foreign objects in the genitourinary system and rectum is made if these objects have been discovered during the course of the examination. Pregnancy tests are made in cases of adolescent girls.

The purpose of the medical examination is to provide substantial evidence that abuse has taken place. The examiner is not responsible for identifying who may have been involved in the incestuous relationship. Therefore, the medical examiner avoids a "whodunit" approach and does not become involved in confronting the family member who may have been named as the perpetrator. If the father is confronted with the child's accusations, he may inflict serious injury on the child as a form of retribution. Therefore, a confrontation must be postponed until measures can be taken to protect the child from the possibility of some form of retaliation by the parent.

The examiner should provide a careful examination of the victim even if the particular incident is said to have happened a long time ago. Because the incident under investigation is usually part of a continuing pattern of behavior rather than an isolated incident, the examiner proceeds on the assumption that the child has probably been exposed to sexual abuse over an extended period of time. Sgroi points out that the physical examination is important in providing legal protection for incest victims:

"These examinations usually constitute the only means by which corroborating evidence of sexual abuse can be collected . . . It is unrealistic to suppose that the child victim's allegations of sexual abuse by an adult, in the absence of any corroborating evidence, will carry a great deal of weight. This is especially true of very young children. In most cases, the younger the child, the greater the need to corroborate her story."[8] Sgroi cautions that the examiner should always proceed as if every case coming to his or her attention will actually be taken to court and that the evidence will be needed to protect the child from further abuse.

If the medical examination is to serve this purpose, the physician must contact the police or protective service worker to report the findings. Some physicians are reluctant to inform authorities in cases of incest, because they think that the family and the child will be subjected to further investigation, with little likelihood that a satisfactory solution to the problem will be worked out, and that the family will be alienated if police are brought into the picture. However, there is a possibility that the parents will be made aware of the serious implications of the sexual abuse if it is reported and that they will take steps to end it. As Leaman points out, "An aspect of the police role which is frequently overlooked is the deterrent influence generated through the fact of police involvement. This influence may be particularly important in cases in which there is a possibility of child neglect or those in which the parent seems to be protecting the suspected offender. If the police are brought into the case even if there is insufficient evidence to prosecute, the parent may make more strenuous efforts to protect the child in order to avoid further police involvement."[9]

The Court Procedure

Prosecuting charges of incest in open court can be a very difficult and painful experience for the victims and their families. The stress that is involved in the course of the trial may actually be more damaging than the incest experience itself. Delays during the proceedings interrupt school schedules, and the normal activities of the family are suspended because the family is preoccupied with legal entanglements and the outcome of the trial. More and more time is devoted to the court procedure as the trial gets underway, the relationships between family members are undermined, and the family begins to feel the pressure of the situation in all aspects of their day-to-day living.

During the trial, the victim must relive the incest experience mentally and verbally. The court procedure is unfamiliar and confusing to the child and, even if the prosecutor has made a conscientious effort to prepare the victim beforehand, the strange environment of the court is threatening and intimidating. In cross-examination, the defense counsel may try to discredit the child's testimony by implying that the story has no foundation in fact. The child is often aware that many people share this belief and senses the suspicion that is evident in the courtroom. Confused and intimidated, the child may begin to waver in giving testimony that is needed to make the prosecutor's case. If the testimony fails to be convincing and the child's credibility is undermined, an additional problem is created for the child who returns to the home in which the sexual abuse took place. A victim who returns home under these conditions feels betrayed by those who were promising to protect her against further sexual mistreatment by her father.

Therefore, it is not surprising that many families who have gone through the legal process come away from the experience feeling that is has been more harmful than helpful. A study conducted by the American Humane Society found that more than half of the families reported that the court experience was harmful to the child. The report indicates that although the intent of the law is to protect the child from sexual abuse, the effect is often severely damaging because it disintegrates the family in the process of protecting the child.

Henry Giarretto, who has worked with many incest victims and their families, points out that the criminal justice system is intent on proving that there has been a violation of the law and, in so doing, it "descends on the child and the family with terrifying force." He writes:

> From the clinically detailed police reports, it appears that the only interest in the child is for the testimony she can give toward conviction of the father. The entire family is entangled in the web of retribution. The child is brought to a children's center, often without the mother's knowledge. The father is jailed and the mother must place the family on welfare. In sum, the family is dismembered, rendered destitute and must painfully find its way to unification.[10]

Incest victims are often frightened by the authority of the law and the power it exerts over their lives. If they are brought to the children's shelter and forcibly separated from their families, they feel lonely and threatened despite the attendant's efforts to make the stay at the center relatively pleasant. If the court determines that the mother cannot provide sufficient protection against the father's sexual abuse, the victim may be removed to a foster home and end up convinced that she is the one who is being punished for participating in the incestuous relationship.

A father who is convicted of incest also undergoes a life-shattering experience. Giarretto describes this experience:

> His life savings are wiped out by the lawyer's fees of several thousand dollars. He finds imprisonment extremely painful; from a respected position in society, he has fallen into the lowest social stratum. His fellow inmates call him "baby raper." No one is more despicable. He is segregated and subjected to indignities and violence. His self-loathing is more intense than that of his inmates. He gradually finds some relief in the fervent resolution that, given a chance, he will make it up to his child, wife and family.[11]

The outcome of the legal process also has an adverse impact on the victim's mother. Often, she feels that her family has been destroyed once her husband has been found guilty. She begins to question her adequacy as a mother and blames herself for having permitted the father to have access to the daughter. Her feelings toward her husband are often confused. She is confused between feelings of anger toward him for his behavior, and her recognition that he was in many ways a good father and that the other children need him. She wonders if she would take him back. If she does, she wonders what assurance she will have that he will not repeat the sexual offenses with other daughters. If she allows him to return home, her relatives and friends may believe that she has abandoned her daughter. The child-welfare authorities may refuse to let her daughter return home as long as the husband lives in the same house. She often doubts that the marriage can be made viable and that she and her husband can rebuild their relationship.

Attempts have been made to avoid these harmful consequences by modifying the legal procedure in cases of intra-familial sexual abuse. For example, in Israel, cases of sex abuse of children are turned over to "youth examiners" rather than to police or other legal personnel. The youth examiners are responsibile for obtaining the facts of sexual offense, assessing the effects of the experience on the child and determining whether the case should be passed on for criminal prosecution. The examiner also decides whether the child should be called upon to give testimony. This form of procedure places high priority on the best interest of the child and places less emphasis on the prosecution of the offender.

Berliner and Stevens suggest that the interests of the child could be better served if an advocate were assigned to cases in which a child is called upon as a witness in criminal procedures. This advocate would be a person qualified to speak out for the child in court when questioning is inappropriate to the age and comprehension of the child. Berliner and Stevens point out that the presence of an advocate would offset some of the problems now encountered in cases of incest and other forms of sexual abuse of children. Children are generally required to testify while sitting alone in the witness stand and are asked to speak into a microphone while facing the alleged assailant. Questioning may go on for several hours, and the child is expected to sit quietly throughout the hearing. Many of the questions put to the child are beyond his comprehension, but seldom does the child receive help in clarification or explanation during the course of questioning. The child is subjected to cross-examination by the counsel for the defendant with the purpose of undermining the child's credibility. The prosecutor is sometimes reluctant to object to the defense attorney's questions because he does not want to appear to be overprotective of the child. Judges may refrain from interfering because they might influence the jury. Berliner and Stevens point out that under these conditions the child does not receive a fair hearing. "If our society believes that sexual molestation of children is a serious crime, then it seems that special attention must be given to techniques that can be adopted within the criminal justice system which not only encourage the cooperation of the child witness but at the same time acknowledge the inherent limitations on a child's performance."[12]

The advocate accompanies the child to the interview with the detectives and the prosecutor and informs the victim what is likely to happen once the trial gets underway. The advocate's understanding of the legal system provides protection for the child

through the court proceedings, and the presence of the advocate
shields the child from fears that are associated with the power of
the law. During this time of crisis, the continuing support of the
advocate is an important factor in sustaining the family during
the time when anxiety and confusion produce severe stress for all
who are involved in the legal process. In addition, the advocate
keeps in touch with the prosecutor to make certain that the case
is receiving full attention. " We call the detective and call the prosecutor," write Berliner and Stevens, "to inquire: What is happening,
where is the case, what are you charging, what are your recommendations?" Experience indicates that the use of an advocate is an
effective method for protecting the child and enforcing the law.
When the advocate is present, the daughter is less apt to be intimidated into withdrawing the charges. Therefore, the father is faced
with the possibility of having to stand trial and risk the chance of
being sent to prison. Under these circumstances, some fathers
voluntarily agree to plead guilty rather than go through a legal
contest.

Several other proposals have been put forward as ways of im-
proving the judicial process. One such proposal is the use of pre-
trial bargaining in order to bring the case to an early conclusion
and lessen the emotional stress for the victim and the family that
is associated with protracted court procedures. A higher percentage of cases could be disposed of within a shorter period of time.
If the child has a strong advocate to represent his interests during
the negotiation process, the outcome would be satisfactory and
the need to subject the victim to a hearing before the court would
be eliminated. The use of negotiation and plea bargaining also may
result in a higher probability of conviction than a formal hearing
of the case in most instances. In some instances, the judge has the
option of hearing the case in chambers and thereby avoiding the
stressful situation of requiring the child to testify in open court
about the details of the sexual assault in a public setting. These
procedural reforms could be useful in protecting the child and at
the same time facilitate the conviction of the offender.

Other procedural reforms have to do with the investigation of
the complaint as it is now carried out in most communities. The
child is usually subjected to repeated questioning by a number of

persons, all of whom are seeking the same information. It has been suggested that the redundancy and repetitive questioning could be eliminated if the child's testimony is videotaped, including the defense attorney's cross-examination of the child. The videotape recording could by played in court so that the child would not have to testify in the presence of her father. The constitutionality of this procedure has not yet been tested in the courts, and it may not be possible to substitute this method of trying the defendant on charges of incest. This procedure does have the advantage of interviewing the child immediately after the complaint has been filed and would result in making a stronger case because the child's testimony would be accurate and less distorted than testimony given several months after the events occurred.

There are also those who contend that the arbitrary "age of consent" set out by law in many states is in need of change. The law places certain limitations on the charges that can be filed against the father depending on the age of the daughter. Usually, the age of consent ranges from puberty to late adolescence. If the sexual offense takes place after the age of consent, the father is charged with incest only if he used physical force or threats of physical force. The issue centers on whether the child who is dependent on the father is really free to give consent to an incestuous involvement at any age. Because of the very nature of the relationship between the perpetrator and the victim, Herman points out that the use of parental power to gain access to the child should be recognized as a criminal form of coercion regardless of the age of the child.

Therapeutic versus Judicial Approaches

Because of the difficulties involved in the legal prosecution of sex offenders, several communities have begun to develop treatment programs of the offender as an alternative to conviction and imprisonment. Judges have the option to require that the offender who is found guilty enter treatment as an alternative to going to prison. The judge can place the father on probation on the condition that he cooperate fully in the treatment program, and the power of the court can be exercised by the probation officer who is responsible for seeing that the order for mandatory treatment is carried out. If the father fails to comply with the court order, he can be given a prison sentence.

A program designed to coordinate the efforts of law enforcement agencies and offer a nonpunitive form of intervention in cases of incest has been established in Santa Clara, California. Based on the principles of humanistic psychology, the Child Sexual Abuse Treatment Program (CSATP), discussed in Chapter Four, works with the criminal justice system to provide an alternative to the traditional approach of punishing the offender. The program is directed toward the rehabilitation of the family in order to protect the victim from further sexual abuse. Henry Giarretto, founder of the CSATP, believes that his treatment approach is effective in cases of incestuous behavior. He writes:

> When incestuous behavior is occurring within a family, each family member is very apt to feel burdened by the 'not good enough' label. Denigration, angry diatribes and punishment do not improve past conduct. Instead, they produce a defensive backlash that deters progress. To intervene creatively in this situation, it is necessary to forget about labels and instead meet the person nonjudgementally.[12]

Giarretto points out that this humanistic approach can be incorporated into the criminal justice system through the establishment of a coordinated community program for the treatment of incest offenders. The CSATP center is a successful attempt to put his idea into practice. Strong emphasis is placed on maintaining the family integrity and reuniting families whenever possible. To achieve these goals, the staff has actively enlisted the cooperation of law enforcement officials in referring families to the program. In the early stages of development, much of the staff's effort was devoted to enlisting the cooperation of a few prosecutors and judges to permit fathers who were being prosecuted to participate in the program. With a successful track record established, more officials in the criminal justice system are referring cases to CSATP.

Experience has shown that the authority of the criminal justice system is essential to keep families involved in treatment. Most of the families that dropped out of the program were not referred by police or courts. Experience also indicates that the family must feel that getting involved in treatment will be helpful and that the entire family will benefit from participating in the program. The humanistic approach to the problem of incest provides a creative alternative to the traditional use of punitive action that is found in most communities. "Families are reconstituted rather than fragmented," Giarretto explains. "Child victims are more likely to become productive adults, and offenders are returned to society as responsible citizens rather than banished to the outlaw subculture."

The issue of whether the treatment approach to incest is as effective as legal solutions to the problem has been examined by Kroth and associates, who conducted a study comparing the CSATP program to that of the Child Welfare Services Department of Sacramento County, which provides limited social services in the treatment of incest cases. Under this plan, a protective service worker investigates the complaint and can remove the child from the home for seventy-two hours. During this period, the family can agree to become involved in voluntary counseling. However, the worker can also file a petition in the juvenile court and begin the formal process of investigation to prove that the allegations set forth in the petition are true. The case is then heard in the juvenile court. If the court sustains the petition, two options are available. The first option is to place the child under the supervision of the court and return the child to the home of her parents. The protective service worker is responsible for the child's safety and has the authority to remove the child from the home at any time. The second option is to place the child in a foster home after the allegations have been sustained by the court. The protective service worker is then responsible for supervising the child's care and for attempts to help the child's parents resolve their problem through ongoing counseling.

The differences in how these two counties approach the incest problem offer some interesting contrasts. The Sacramento approach appears to emphasize child protection and conviction of the offender. Therefore, considerable money and effort is expended in the investigation of complaints rather than in providing therapy. On the other hand, the Santa Clara program overcomes the need for extensive investigation by gaining the family's cooperation in family therapy. Because of this difference in approach, Kroth found that the Santa Clara program probably reaches more cases of incest because the judicial investigative procedure "scares off" reports of sexual abuse in families. The study showed that CSATP received 22 percent more cases of incest than the Sacramento Child Welfare Services Department. The report concluded that Sacramento County could be missing as many as 37 percent of all incest cases, and, at an annual rate, the number of missed victims could be as high as 64. The investigative justice system approach therefore exposed 64 victims to continuing sexual abuse because it did not have a highly developed way of encouraging families to enter into therapy and rehabilitation. Kroth observes that "intrafamilies sexual abuse is far more protected than extrafamilies abuse and the coercive elements within the family structure may operate to keep the sexual abuse secret, allowing the duration of the abuse to continue for many years without coming to attention." [13]

Cooperation with Social Services

The criminal justice system is an important component in the network of services available to incest victims and their families, but the effectiveness of the legal approach to sexual abuse depends on close cooperation with professional personnel in other fields such as medicine, mental health and social work. Coordination of legal services with other community agencies has proved to be an effective method of providing an alternative to the incarceration of offenders and a more enlightened approach to the problem of incest by prosecuting attorneys and judges.

To achieve the goal of an integrated effort to protect incest victims, several communities have developed programs that provide a structure for the coordination of services. The Child Guidance and Evaluation Center at Austin, Texas has established a Community Resource Network Project that enables the local child-protection agency, the local police department and the district attorney's office to call on the staff at the center to assist in the investigation of complaints in cases of sexual abuse. The center also maintains a program that is designed to integrate the management of cases of child sexual abuse among the various agencies involved in providing services to the victim. Regular monthly meetings are called to evaluate and review cases and to solve problems in delivering services. Representatives of the police department, the county sheriff and the district attorney are included in discussions of cases, as are representatives of the child-protection agency.

To increase law enforcement officials' knowledge about the nature and treatment of incest, the Community Network Project offers consultation and training for police officers and court officials. Center staff members also offer special training programs for the district attorney's office and provide instruction in methods of interviewing children who are victims of sexual abuse. Consultation and training programs are designed to help law enforcement personnel understand the impact of sexual abuse and to work constructively with the families of incest victims. Law enforcement personnel report that these training programs have substantially improved the procedure for investigating sexual abuse complaints and have led to more effective referrals of families for therapeutic intervention and help in coping with the incest crisis.

The initial contact of the victim and the family with law enforcement officials is a critical factor in the outcome of a complaint of sexual abuse. Police officers admit that they do not have sufficient time or expertise to give the emotional support that the victim and the family need at this critical point. To assist police in carrying out these critical legal and mental health responsibilities involved in the initial stage of investigation, the center has developed a standby service on weekends and nights to take emergency statements on request by the police department.

The criminal justice system encounters considerable difficulty in responding to complaints of incest. District attorneys' offices are reluctant to prosecute incest cases because of the problems involved in obtaining evidence and establishing the credibility of the child witness. Coordination with community agencies through the use of collateral contacts and consultation has proven useful in overcoming these obstacles. Active cooperation between the legal system and the service network is especially useful in preparing a case for grand jury invesigation. The district attorney requests that a staff member of the center accompany the child victim at the grand jury hearing and remain while the questioning is underway in order to minimize the trauma to the victim. During the trial, the district attorney also calls upon the center's staff to provide expert testimony and permits a representative from the Network Project to sit with the child during the courtroom trial.

The Network Project has resulted in a higher percentage of success in the prosecution of offenders. In 68 percent of the Network cases that progressed from the filing of a complaint to testimony before the grand jury, the outcome resulted in the district attorney taking action against the offender. In twenty-one cases, the offender pleaded guilty and was placed on probation, and in most cases he was required to seek treatment as a condition of his probation. Close cooperation with the district attorney makes it possible for the cases involved to be handled informally, and the child may not be required to testify in open court or be subjected to cross-examination by the defendant's attorney. At the same time, there is sufficient incentive for the offender to pursue counseling because the court can revoke the probation if he does not actively participate in therapy. The Network Project experiment in Austin has brought about improved cooperation between law enforcement agencies and community organizations and the program points the way toward an effective and comprehensive approach to the management of incest as a community-wide problem.

REFERENCES

1. Herman, J.: *Father-Daughter Incest.* Cambridge, Mass., Harvard U., 1981, p. 163.
2. Ibid.
3. Rush, F.: *The Best Kept Secret.* Philadelphia, Prentice-Hall, 1980, p. 156.
4. Stember, C.: Art therapy. In U.S. Department of Human Resources: *Sexual Abuse of Children.* Washington, D.C., 1980, p. 60.
5. Ibid.
6. Herman, J.: *Father-Daughter Incest,* p. 166.
7. Rush, F.: *The Best Kept Secret,* p. 155.
8. Sgroi, S.: Comprehensive examination for child sexual abuse. In Burgess, A., et al: *Sexual Assault of Children and Adolescents,* Lexington, Mass., Lexington Books, 1978, p. 144.
9. Leaman, K.: Sexual acts against children. In U.S. Department of Human Resources: *Sexual Abuse of Children.* Washington, D.C., 1980, p. 32.
10. Giarretto, H.: Humanistic treatment of father-daugher incest. In U.S. De-

partment of Human Resources: *Sexual Abuse of Children*. Washington, D.C., 1980, p. 39.

11. Berliner, L., and Stevens, D.: Advocating for sexually abused children. In U.S. Department of Human Resources: *Sexual Abuse of Children*. Washington, D.C., 1980, p. 50.

12. Giarretto, H.: Coordinated community treatment of incest. In Burgess, A., et al.: *Sexual Assault of Children and Adolescents*. Lexington, Mass., Lexington Books, 1978, p. 233.

13. Kroth, J.: *Child Sexual Abuse*. Springfield, Thomas, 1979, p. 148.

Chapter 6

LASTING EFFECTS OF INCEST

Mostly I just feel doomed.
There must be someting wrong
with me; it's like I've been
marked. Sometimes I feel like
there's just no point to keep
on living.

An incest victim

THE immediate consequences of incest for the victim and the family are far reaching. All family members are caught up in the events that follow disclosure of the secret relationship, and the crisis that ensues has a devastating impact on their lives. The victim becomes emotionally isolated from other family members. The offender may be expelled from the family. Long-standing relationships are abruptly disrupted. However, the long-term effects of an incestuous relationship can be even more devastating for the victim. In the sections that follow, the lasting effects of various forms of incest will be examined and the problems that victims face in adult life will be explored.

Effects of Father-Daughter Incest

Therapists who have worked with adult victims of father-daughter incest observe that these women have serious difficulties in forming satisfactory relationships with men. Some avoid all contacts with males; others go through a series of intimate relations that turn out to be highly unsatisfactory. Research also indicates that father-daughter incest victims often seek out men who will mistreat them. They seem to be incapable of avoiding situations

138

that result in further victimization. Although they do not actively invite abuse, they are willing to tolerate mistreatment for extended periods. Therapists use the terms *door mat, punching bag* and *dishrag* in describing the passive-dependent aspects of some adult victims. Several explanations for the passivity of these victims have been offered. One view holds that the acceptance of abuse from men is related to the victim's need to prove that men are beasts and that no man is worthy of affection or respect. Other studies indicate that most victims grew up in families in which the mother modeled a pattern of masochism and endured abuse from her husband. The daughters of these mothers may simply have accepted mistreatment as a part of being female. The incest experience to which they were subjected reinforced this view that women must accept abuse from men.

Some adult victims feel that they deserve to be beaten and mistreated by their husbands and lovers because they perceive themselves to be evil and unworthy of affection and respect. Observing that many victims repeatedly become involved in destructive relationships with men, Herman and Hirschman suggest that their masochistic behavior is an attempt to resolve guilt associated with the incest experience:

> Most of the victims were aware that they had experienced some pleasure in the incestuous relationship and had joined with their fathers in a shared hatred of their mothers. This led to feelings of shame, degradation and worthlessness. Because they had enjoyed their father's attention and their mother's defeat, these women felt responsible for the incestuous situation. Almost uniformly, they distrusted their own desires and needs and did not feel entitled to care and respect.[1]

Therapists have also found that adult victims of father-daughter incest have serious sexual problems that include promiscuity, prostitution and orgasmic dysfunctioning. Meiselman found that 87 percent of the female victims had problems in one or more of these areas at some time after the incest occurred. Of these, 19 percent had gone through a period of promiscuity or were still actively promiscuous many years after incest had ended. Several theories have been proposed to explain the daughter's promiscuous behavior as a result of the incestuous relation with her father. One author suggests that the purpose of the daughter's promiscuity is to relive the experience with her father and to achieve restitution of the lost parent figure. Another author suggests that the daughter acts out her hostility to her parents, particularly her mother, by becoming involved in a series of sexual relationships.

Some therapists perceive the victim's promiscuity as something other than revenge or a compulsion to reenact the incestuous experience. They theorize that these victims sexualize all relationships with men because they are unable to differentiate between sex and affection. Due to their childhood experience, they are confused about the meaning of parental love as different from sexual interaction.

Some victims may use their frequent sexual adventures to prove that men only use women to satisfy their sexual needs and that women are helpless to prevent men from sexually exploiting them. But other victims turn to prostitution after the incest experience. The likelihood of becoming a prostitute is increased if the victim was rewarded with gifts for fulfilling her father's requests for sexual favors. The following is an account of why some victims become prostitutes.

> I knew that, wherever I went, men would find me and abuse me. So, my attitude toward prostitution was, "Why not?" If I had to have sex, I thought, why not get something for it? I felt that I deserved the money; other men were going to have to pay for every time my father had me.
>
> Prostitution was a way for me to capitalize on what I thought was the only thing I had to offer and it was another way of expressing my rage, of getting back at men for what had been done to me. I saw men as suckers who were gong to have to pay for their weakness and desperation. I saw them only in terms of fifty or a hundred dollars. I saw them as anything, except people.

Women who have been badly used by their fathers when they were children may turn to prostitution because they can exercise power over men, just as their fathers had used their power to exploit them sexually. Making men pay for sex was a form of control that the victim could use to her own advantage. As one victim explained: "Since I thought that the only thing men wanted was sex, the only way I could see to get power in a relationship was by making them pay for it. It was my only control, and I could keep it as long as men didn't mean anything to me. Once I cared for them, I felt they had all the control." The role of the prostitute also recapitulated their sexual experience with their fathers in some instances. As child victims, they had disassociated themselves from the sexual act with their fathers. As prostitutes, they also could maintain a detached and highly impersonal relationship with men. "I learned to detach my mind from my body at such an early age that it was easy for me to disassociate myself from those brief sexual encounters," one victim explained. "I thought that other girls were stupid to give it away. I wanted to make lots of money and get rich so I wouldn't need anyone anymore — not my family, my destructive friends, or men."

Another major sexual problem for father-daughter incest victims is orgasmic dysfuntioning, ranging from "selective frigidity" to frigidity in all sexual relationships. Although it is possible that incest may be used as a convenient excuse for lack of sexual response by some women, there is little doubt that, for many victims, sexual experiences arouse strong feelings of repulsion and guilt connected with childhood sexual contacts with their fathers. The following case illustrates how the incest experience can cause problems in sexual functioning for the victim as an adult:

> Dianna was only twenty when she was seen in therapy for marital problems that were partially related to the lack of orgasmic response to her husband of two years. She reported no sexual interest in boys during adolescence, although her future husband had insisted on having premarital relations with her. She described these relations with distaste and conveyed the impression that she endured them only to prove her love for him. Her aversion to sex continued throughout her marriage.

Incest victims who are experiencing problems of orgasmic dysfunctioning explain the source of the problem in various ways. Some trace their lack of sexual response to the fact that they imagine their fathers are watching while they are engaging in sexual intercourse. These victims appear to have a very clear memory of the incestuous experience and carry over a mental image of their fathers into adult life. This mental imagery interferes with the enjoyment of sex relations with lovers and husbands. Other victims become anxious if they experience pleasure in lovemaking because of the guilt feelings associated with having sex with their fathers. When she is having intercourse with her husband, a victim may relive the sexual experience with her father. As one woman explained: "I remember my first year of marriage. I couldn't understand why I didn't like to make love. Then one day it dawned on me when my husband was touching me on the shoulder and I said, 'That feels just like what my father did to me and I can't stand it.' It was repelling to me. I couldn't stand the feeling of my father's skin against my skin. I would just get a creepy-crawly feeling when he would touch me."

Another father-daughter incest victim, age twenty-six, was sexually active in a series of short-term relations with men during college, but she was unable to be responsive in sexual intercourse. She related her sexual dysfunctioning to her incestuous experience as follows:

> The sexual dysfunctioning that I have to this day is attributable to my relationship with my father. The sexual dysfunctioning that came from it was that for so many years I had made myself so rigid and unresponsive that it's very difficult for me to respond, to relax in a sexual situation, because the most familiar feeling is still being oriented to please but to be completely rigid and closed within myself.
>
> To this day, if I'm not feeling really okay, I will still perform sex as a service. What happens with penetration is that if I'm not relaxed, it's painful to me. What happens in those situations is that the pain is experienced as my just deserts. It's masochistic.[2]

The sexual dysfuntioning of these victims is difficult to overcome, but the use of sensate-focus exercises and relaxation strategies can be helpul in overcoming negative feelings and developing a capacity for positive sexual response.

Depression is one of the most common psychological aftereffects of incest. The depression is sometimes caused by guilt feelings when the victims blame themselves for having been involved in incestuous behavior. Looking back on the incestuous experience, adult victims condemn themselves for not having resisted the sexual advances of a father or brother. Most victims also think that they are tainted, damaged and worthless because they engaged in sexual contacts with family members during their childhood or adolescence. The shame that attaches to incest adds to the depth of the victim's depression and low self-esteem. Various forms of self-destructive behavior often accompany the depression, as illustrated in the following account of a woman who was sexually abused by her father.

> I felt so doomed that I often thought I might as well shorten the agony. I was very young the first time I tried to overdose on a bottle of aspirin. Mostly I tried to overdose on drugs but sometimes I did other things like cut my wrists. Sometimes I was relieved to wake up hoping that others would finally see how bad things had gotten for me. Other times, I was bitterly disappointed to find that I was still alive.

The incest can also result in victims inflicting severe physical pain on their bodies. One woman recalls that her anger about being sexually abused by her father was turned against herself and she resorted to several forms of self-mutilation to discharge her feelings.

> I felt such rage that I had to hurt someone. So I'd hurt myself because I hated myself for being so powerless. I also wanted to be tough — to show others that nothing could hurt me anymore. It gave me a sense of self-worth. My tolerance for pain increased, and the physical pain I inflicted on myself acted as a release for the emotional pain I couldn't express. I burned myself from my wrists to my elbows with a cigarette. I still have the scars today.

Feelings of distrust of men are prevalent among women who have been involved in father-daughter incest. Having been betrayed by their fathers, they expect all men to be untrustworthy. The distrust affects their relationships to men, as this victim explains: "My initial reaction to advances by a male is usually that they are just out for what they can get. On the other hand, I will often get involved in a sexual liaison where I know that that's what's going on. I'll do it, and I know that I'll feel bad when it is over, and I still do it. I consider men as selfish creatures who only want from me what they can get."

Therapists point out that in some cases the victim who has strong feelings of distrust about men forms relationships that reinforce her perception that all men are unreliable and exploitative.

To relieve pain and loneliness, many daughters turn to alcohol and other drugs. Drug abuse is also part of a tortuous form of self-destruction. One victim reported that she used various drugs indiscriminately, not caring what she swallowed, and that she purposely used dirty needles in order to contract hepatitis. Alcohol is also used as an outlet for self-destructive behavior. As one victim explains: "I got more physically self-destructive when I was drinking. I could tolerate more physical pain when I was drunk. I had been drinking when I burned my arms and during several suicide attempts."

The consequences that result from incest take various forms: depression, low self-esteem, problems in relationships with men, distrust and self-destructive behavior. But all these aftereffects have a common origin in the childhood experiences of the victims. The Justices point out that all these problems in adult life grow out of the kind of parenting the victim receives in incestuous families. In incestuous families, the roles of parent and child are reversed. The incest victim is forced into the adult role and assumes responsibility for keeping the family united by becoming the family scapegoat. "Because many take a position of being responsible for their parents instead of their parents being responsible for them, these children never receive the kind of love and nurturing necessary for healthy growth and development," explain the Justices. "They feel abandoned and experience a lack of being part of a 'real' family. They struggle, sometimes all their lives, to get that nurturing and a feeling of belonging and being cared for."[3]

Victims of father-daughter incest who marry and have young children fear that the husband will sexually abuse their daughters. Some become very suspicious of their husband's relationship with their daughters. One mother who had become pregnant by her father eventually told her husband about the incest. The husband described his wife as a very nervous individual who suffered from insomnia. She was sexually unresponsive but was fond of her husband. The husband observed that she was extremely suspicious about his relationship to the children. "She watches me like a hawk with those kids," he said. "She doesn't want me to be too loving with them and to be too open about sex. It makes her think of her father." Another incest victim who is the mother of two prepubescent children went to work to support them, leaving them in the care of the man with whom she was living. She found out that when she was away from home, her lover not only abused them physically but he also forced them to have oral sex. "I cry a lot," she says, "because I think that I should have been able to see that didn't happen to my own children. They should not have to go through the same thing I did when I was their age. I can picture myself in my daughter at her age, what I went through, and I realize now I can't change any of it."

Women who have been past victims of incest report that they do not want to have any children because they fear that they might transmit it to another generation. There is some evidence that sexual abuse can be transmitted because sexually abused girls sometimes select abusive partners and may fail to protect their own children against sexual abuse. Several factors may bring about such a passing on of incest. A woman who has been subjected to incest sees this as a pattern of parenting that is not desirable. Yet, she chooses a man who turns to the daughter for sex because that is the only kind of man to whom she can relate. When the marriage does not fulfill the expectations of the victim, she may abandon her roles as a responsible parent because she finds that her own needs for nurturing are not being met by her husband. Research also indicates that there is a possibility that parents who were sexually abused as children are likely to physically and emotionally abuse their own offspring. A study that was conducted at Cedar House in Long Beach, California indicated that 90 percent of the mothers who were seen there for help relating to child abuse had been sexually abused as children. The mothers of these abused children were known to be currenlty involved in a sexual relationship with the man in the house, a neighbor or a friend. The Justices also found that among the cases of physical abuse of children that came to their attention there was a background of sexual abuse in the parents.

Because it is difficult to systematically follow the lives of incest victims over an extended period, the nature and extent of harm that is caused by incestuous relationships are quite imprecise. Moreover, no substantial information has been obtained by comparing children from incestuous families to children who have grown up in nonincestuous families that have similar socioeconomic and family backgrounds. Without such a study that includes a control group, the exact extent of damage caused by incest cannot be determined with a high degree of certainty. Nevertheless, most clinicians and researchers believe that children who are victims of incest also suffer some degree of emotional trauma. As the Justices point out, "There is no doubt that some children will make it through the incestuous experience with fewer scars than others just as some soldiers make it through the war with fewer wounds. Nevertheless, few people live through the experience of incest or war without some scars."[4]

Effects of Brother-Sister Incest

Social scientists believe that sibling incest is more common than father-daughter incest, although it is less frequently reported. Because brothers and sisters are closer in age than parents and children, less stigma is attached to sibling sexual contacts. The sexual interaction most often begins with curiosity about sex and in some cases develops into an extended period of mutual acceptance of sexual intercourse between brother and sister. In a few cases, sisters report that the sexual activity was pleasurable, but most describe it as annoying and bothersome. They usually resent the brother for having initiated it. If the brother and sister are about the same age and if the incestuous activity grew out of a normal curiosity, the sister does not find the experience highly repulsive. However, if the brother is several years older and if he uses his sister as a primary outlet for his sexual urges, the girl is likely to find the experience highly impersonal and exploitative. Older brothers are usually inclined to introduce the sexual activity abruptly and in some instances use threats or force to make the sister comply with their sexual demands, as illustrated in the case of Karen who was sexually abused by a brother who was nine years her senior.

To all outward appearances, Karen's family was a normal American family. Both parents were well educated and held important jobs. Karen's father was absent from the home most of the time because his work required that he travel extensively. Therefore, he was not aware of what was happening while he was gone from home. Karen's mother worked until half-past five in the evenings, and Henry, the oldest child, was put in charge of the younger brother and sister until their mother came home from work. It was during the afternoon, between the time that school was over and before the mother returned home, that the incest took place. Karen was six years old when her brother, Henry, age fifteen, initated sexual activity. She recalls that Henry would lock the younger brother out of the house before he assaulted her. "I remember it always took place in the bathroom. I can remember bleeding and crying when he forced me to have sexual intercourse. One time, or maybe several times, he made me do it orally, and that was the most repulsive because it meant that I had to participate in sex with him. Otherwise, I could go into the wall, just not be aware of what was happening, shut off my mind while he had sex with me," Karen said. "It was rape and it continued until he left home to go to college. So it lasted for almost four years. And up to this day, I can't stand the smell of semen."

"I also remember the times when he threatened to beat me up if I cried," Karen continued. "And there were a lot of bruises on my body where he had hurt me. I tried to get away from him by hiding or going to the neighbors, but then he would tell my mother I didn't come home and I would be in trouble. I was very scared and ashamed. In junior high, I wouldn't take showers with the rest of the girls because I thought they would find out what was happening at home. I thought everybody could see that I was 'spoiled,' that I wasn't a normal person and that I was doing something wrong. I knew it was wrong, even though I didn't have any way of judging on the basis of sound information about sex. But I did know that it had to be kept secret, and so I thought there must be something wrong about it. My parents never talked about sex at anytime that I can ever remember. Even after I got to college, I still thought that I might get pregnant from the intercourse my brother had with me. I didn't know that the sperm only lived a short time. So I was always afraid that once the sperm got inside it stayed there and could make me pregnant even though the incest had stopped a year or more ago."

Another victim of brother-sister incest recalls that she was six years old when the first incident occurred. Her brother was about age thirteen when he raped her during this first sexual encounter. He told her: "I'm going to do something. It's okay, but if you ever tell anybody you know what I can do. But you are going to like it." The sexual activity took place regularly once per week. She remembers crying and experiencing pain, and she also became terrified of becoming pregnant. "I just lived in constant fear most of my life," she said. "I just didn't know which way to turn, where to hide, what to do. At the same time I didn't know how I could stop it. All I know is that from the time I was six until I was sixteen, every day of my life, I just wanted to die."

The following account of an incest victim who was only three when the first episode of sexual activity occurred illustrates how the incestuous behavior begins because of sexual curiosity and continues over several years. Her brother came to her and suggested that they play doctor. She does not remember all the details, but she remembers the pain, the terror and the guilt. "My brother was really rough on me," she said. "He was much bigger than I was. As a little six-year-old you don't have any moisture or anything. It was very painful. It really hurt. I didn't yell. I kept all that inside. I didn't tell because I was too terrified. And because I felt guilty." She recalls that there was no one to whom she could reveal her terror and guilt. "I can remember just crying and crying and crying. And nobody ever sat down with me and said, 'Little girl, what's the matter?' Nobody. Never, never, never."

Several factors are responsible for sex play developing into a highly erotic attachment that eventually takes the form of sexual intercourse between siblings. The absence of the father, or his limited ability to exercise control over the behavior of the son, is a contributing factor because there is no power figure that can effectively restrain the brother from misusing his sister. Fatherless families, in which the older brother takes on the role of the head of the family and has considerable power, are especially susceptible to brother-sister incest. The role of the mother in defining appropriate behavior is equally important. Mothers deal with sex education of their children in various ways. Some give their daughters the impression that sex is bad and lecture them about its evils. Under these conditions, the siblings carry out their sexual behavior without letting their mother know what is happening. On the other hand, there are mothers who are not really concerned about their children's sexual behavior. Weinberg refers to "loose sex culture" in some families as a factor in brother-sister incest and suggests that parents in these families do not supervise the children's sexual activity because they are unconcerned about it. The sexual climate in these families is very permissive. Children see their parents engage in sexual intercourse or know that their parents are sexually promiscuous. Weinberg's study also indicates that brother-sister incest occurred after the brother knew that his sister had been involved in sex with his father.[5]

Most sisters do not disclose a sexual relation with their brothers to their mothers, and brothers seem to assume that their sister will not tell adults about the sexual activity for fear of being punished for her part in the relationship, particularly if she has been cooperative and does not strongly resist his advances. In contrast to father-daughter incest, brother-sister affairs usually do not continue beyond a few incidents, because the sister can more easily terminate the behavior when she loses interest and wants to direct her sexual activity outside the family. The victims of brother-sister incest sometimes assume that the mother knows about the relationship but does nothing to stop it, as illustrated in the following comments: "I looked to my mother to protect me, but she just didn't want to see what was going on with my brother. I think she could have asked some questions. After all, there were bruises and bleeding. But I never told her and she never asked any questions."

Another incest victim tried to tell her mother that she was being sexually abused by her brother, but the mother did not believe her: "One time I tried telling my mother this: 'You know I wish you wouldn't go out. Bobbie doesn't treat me right when you go out.' And she said, 'What do you mean?' And then I said, 'Well, you know he is too rough on us.' And she said, 'That can't be. He's not like that.' Because he wasn't to her. I mean he could be a very charming young man." The long-term effects of sibling incest have been examined by several researchers who have compared the adult adjustment of sisters to the adjustment of daughters as adults. Weinberg found that sisters were better adjusted and were less likely to become promiscuous in sexual relationships in adult life. Kubo concluded that women involved in sex with their brothers were less apt to develop serious emotional and mental disturbances than those involved in sex with fathers. Lukianowicz came to a similar conclusion in his study of incest victims as adults. Meiselman studied the marital adjustment of sisters and found that adult sisters tended to have more stable marital histories than daughters. However, the study indicated that many of them suffered passively in marriages that were very unsatisfactory over a long period of time. Meiselman found that generally the adult sisters were not completely alienated from their brothers, but they did continue to distrust them.

There are indications that sisters have serious problems in sexual adjustment as adults. Meiselman reports that 85 percent failed to achieve orgasm or achieved it only in very unusual circumstances that involved masochistic forms of sexual interaction. If the sister voluntarily entered into incest with her brother, she would not be apt to be masochistic in her relationships with men, but rather to be more inclined to engage in a number of sexual relationships in adult life. In those cases where the brother used force to involve the sister, she was inclined to view the incest as a form of mistreatment and accept masochistic relationships because she felt helpless during the childhood and adolescent years. When the sister reaches young-adult life, she may realize the full impact of the incestuous relationship with her brother, as in the following statement of a woman who was sexually abused by her brother beginning when she was six years old:

> I have no hope of ever having a meaningful relationship to a male; the nightmares are still with me; I still have difficulty thinking I am worthy of anyone's friendship. I never did consider marriage because of the sex thing. I felt I could never become involved with a man who didn't know that something had taken place in my life.

I mean, definitely, I was not a virgin. And I just felt that someday I'd have to explain if I ever got to that point.

The aftereffects of sibling incest may take the form of depression and anxiety in adult life for some victims:

A year after my brother left home and the relationship stopped, I was relieved. But then in my freshman year of college, I tried to commit suicide. I just felt that my whole world was falling apart. Now I am not really depressed, but I have nightmares. I am afraid that someone will break into my bedroom, and I run out in the living room trying to see if anyone is there. It is like I am trying to escape from someone.

The aftereffects of sibling incest are less serious and damaging to the victim if she and her brother were about the same age when the sexual activity took place. When the brother is considerably older than the victim, there is a greater likelihood that force has been used and that the experience will produce trauma that carries over into adult life.

Uncle-Niece Incest

The Kinsey study of female sexual behavior indicated that uncle-niece sexual relationships were quite common among the women included in the sample. Apparently, the vast majority of these women did not experience severe trauma in view of the fact they did not seek psychotherapy for disturbances related to sexual activity with their uncles. The experience may be less disturbing to these incest victims, because the uncle usually obtains the cooperation of the niece in a gentle way and because there is no strong relationship between the incest partners. The typical incident with an uncle does not seriously disrupt family relationships as does father-daughter incest and, therefore, it is less damaging to the victim. However, if the uncle used force, the experience has a strong impact on a young child, as in the following case.

Donna's incestuous relationship with her uncle began when she was about three years old. The uncle, who was about twenty-two years old at the time, lived alone with his mother, Donna's grandmother, in a city on the East coast. Donna would go to visit her grandmother during the summer months when school was in recess and return to her parents' home in the fall. Her parents did not know that the incest was happening. Donna did try to tell her grandmother that her uncle was sexually abusing her, but she had difficulty finding the words to describe what her uncle was doing. "I would tell my grandmother that he was doing bad things to me. She would say, 'Well, does he hit you,' and I would say, 'No, but he does bad things.' My uncle never did beat me up. He would just use threats to keep me from telling anyone what was going on, and so I didn't try to say anything more about it." The incest continued until Donna was about eight years old. When her parents decided not to send her to her grandmother's home, the relation with the uncle broke off. She has had no contact with him since that time.

During early adolescence, Donna went through several transitions in her relationship to men. She recalls that other girls regarded her as "a real prude" and that she kept "fending boys off all the time." She had many fears that were related to the incestuous experience, but she did not realize the exact connection between her anxiety and what had happened earlier in her life. "It was a matter of pushing things down, I just tried not thinking about things." In her sophomore year, she fell in love with a man who was very kind to her, but she could not respond to him sexually. When the relationship ended after two years, Donna became depressed and engaged in a series of sexual relationships. "I didn't really know what was going on in my mind at the time. But now that I look back, I think that was the only way I knew how to make contact with men," she said. "I would either relate to men only on an intellectual level or on a sexual level. The kind of men I would pick were either real sweet, men who I could control and who were not really my equal, or I would pick men who were tough and who would really hurt me by the way they treated me. But I saw them as strong. I would always end up having an affair if the relationship began to become stable or permanent."

Fortunately, Donna has been able to work through her relationship wth men satisfactorily and is now looking forward to marriage. She has also completed her graduate work and is well on the way to a professional career. But not all women who have been sexually abused by their uncles are this fortunate. Meiselman describes a case in which the victim was three years old when an uncle injured her vagina so badly that she had to be treated in a hospital, but the girl's mother refused to acknowledge that the uncle's sexual behavior was a serious problem. The niece, now in her forties, is still angry at the mother for not protecting her. In another case, a twelve-year-old girl was persuaded to have intercourse with her twenty-one-year-old uncle. Two years later, she was approached by the uncle's forty-five-year-old father and had intercourse with him on several occasions. At the age of forty she entered psychotherapy for treatment of numerous marital problems.

Two factors are important in determining the extent of trauma that results from incest between an uncle and niece. If the uncle is considerably older than the victim, the incestuous relationship is similar to father-daughter incest. A twenty-six-year-old uncle who bribes or threatens his eight-year-old niece into having a sexual relationship is exposing her to a harmful experience. If the uncle lives in the same household as the niece, the relationship parallels father-daughter incest in that the uncle is perceived to be an adult who acts in a parental role. If the child's contacts with the uncle are infrequent, the child does not feel that daily survival depends on the uncle, and the trauma is less severe and produces few lasting effects.

Grandfather-Granddaughter Incest

Grandfather-Granddaughter incest is a form of extended family incest that has received attention from professionals who have worked with incest victims. They have found that the popular stereotype of the incestuous grandfather as a "dirty old man" who is mentally defective is not supported by the facts. They observe that incestuous grandfathers have many of the same doubts about their masculinity as do incestuous fathers. Troubled by the aging process, they do not feel as powerful or competent as they once were. In some cases, they are relegated to the role of baby-sitter and have easy access to the granddaughter. Many grandfathers also lack attention and affection. The granddaughter is often very affectionate and trusting. The grandfather can exploit this situation if he is so inclined.

One victim recalled that she was molested by her grandfather during her early childhood. When she was about four years old, her grandfather took her into his bedroom on the pretext of taking a nap and then removed some of her clothing and fondled her genitals. These incidents were repeated frequently for more than a year. The grandfather would give her gifts, and she enjoyed the special attention he gave her. However, as an adult, she felt guilty about the sexual contacts and blamed herself for her grandfather's behavior. She became extremely religious and experienced serious sexual problems in her marriage. Another woman who sought psychotherapy because of sexual problems recalled that her grandfather engaged in genital manipulation with her on numerous occasions between the ages five to ten. In later yers she felt guilty about the incestuous behavior with her grandfather. Most grandfathers are gentle in their approach and do not use force or intimidate the victim. Therefore, this form of incestuous relationship usually does not produce serious trauma or have severely damaging consequences in the adult life of the granddaughter.

Mother-Son Incest

Incest between mother and son is generally regarded as the most rare and highly taboo form of incestuous behavior. Actual sexual intercourse is seldom reported; the sexual activity more often consists of fondling and exposure, washing the child's genitals to stimulation, the son sleeping with the mother past the age when it is appropriate, massaging the son to erection and undressing in the same room.

The conditions that lead to mother-son incest have been outlined by researchers who have examined those few cases that came to the attention of authorities or psychotherapists. Role reversal appears to be an integral part of the dynamics. The father is usually absent from home and in his absence the son takes his place as head of the family. The son tries to fill the void left by the father, may sleep with the mother to alleviate her fears at night and develop a close emotional and physical attachment to her. The mother's needs are more emotional than sexual, but the situation becomes sexually stimulating to the son. He may become involved in sexual fantasies about his mother, and she then becomes the sole object of his erotic feelings and sexual desires.

When the mother initiates the incest relationship, she generally creates a strong relationship of emotional dependence between herself and the victim. The mother concentrates her affection on the son and deters him from social and sexual contacts with other women. In turn, the son becomes socially dependent on his mother, and eventually the close relationship involves one or more forms of sexual interaction with the mother, as illustrated in this case study.

Fred's mother bathed or helped him bathe until he was fifteen. As he matured, he became more sexually aroused when the mother frequently fondled him. He then began to fondle his mother. He had never gone with a girl until he was twenty-eight years old. His mother warned him against women, telling him that they would take his money, and he implicitly believed her. Fred's mother had complete control over his life, and after her third marriage ended in divorce, the relationship between her and Fred became highly intimate. They slept in the same room and saw each other in the nude. The mother encouraged Fred's sexual attraction to her and later asked him to sleep with her.

When the son is the aggressor in the incestuous behavior, the mother may try to be sexually distant from him. In most cases, the son is aware that his mother is sexually promiscuous and may cease to defer to her as his mother because of her sexual behavior. The mother is also indifferent to the sexual behavior of the children, and although she is opposed to having sexual relationships with her son, she indirectly encourages his sexual aggression by her open promiscuity. The following case study illustrates how an incestuous relationship may develop under these conditions. Both the mother and son were sexually promiscuous, and the son had seen his mother entertaining men in her home as a professional prostitute. The mother often teased her son because she never saw him with girls. The son became angry and asked his mother to have intercourse with him, because he felt that if other men had intercourse with her he should also have that right. He attempted to have sex with her when she had fallen asleep and demanded she fulfill her promise that perhaps sometime she would "let me have it too."

Mother-initiated incest appears to be related to psychopathology in the mother. This form of incest usually falls short of actual sexual intercourse, but it has been known to occur when the son is between the ages of ten to eighteen. Most mothers who initiate sex with their sons are unstable neurotic women who are unable to relate to men and tend to have a background of sexual promiscuity and heavy drinking. Reports of son-initiated incest suggest that the son is typically very disturbed at the time of the incest attempts and that the incest is generally seen as a continuation of an emotional disorder which allows sexual fantasies to be carried out. Some clinicians have speculated that incest produces psychotic symptoms in the sons. Meiselman points out that the symptoms may be the cause rather than the result of incest. She writes: "It appears that mother-son incest is seldom an important factor in schizophrenia. In many cases, the son is schizophrenic at the time of incest and also afterward, but it seems that the son's gross personality disturbance and lack of ego control allow an incestuous approach to the mother to be made."[6]

Homosexual Incest

The most commonly reported form of homosexual incest is sexual activity between father and son. It appears that the father is always the initiator of the sexual behavior and that many of them have had strong homosexual desires since early childhood. They have usually witnessed incestuous behavior in their family of origin or have been victims of sexual abuse as children. The incest may begin with fondling, mutual masturbation and oral-genital contact or exposure. The sons are often too young to understand the sexual nature of the activity. Fathers present the sexual interaction to their sons as an expression of affection. They are usually strongly attached to their sons. The sons do not resist the fathers' sexual advances because they want to please. If the son becomes alienated as a result of the incest, the father may become guilt-ridden and depressed. The impact on the son is twofold. The experience presents problems for sexual identity because the primary sexual experience has been with a male rather than with a female. Therefore, ths son who is sexually abused by his father does not have the normal exposure to girls during his growing-up years in order to discover his own sexuality. The confusion over sexual identity may become a serious concern in adolescence or early adult years because the son fears that he may become homosexual. Because of his homosexual fears the victim of father-son incest may have some difficulty in achieving a satisfactory sexual adjustment in adult life.

Homosexual relations between mothers and daughters are the most understudied area of research. The literature contains almost no case studies of such incestuous relations, indicating that they are very rare or seldom reported. The mother who involves her daughter in an incestuous relation seems to rely on her daughter for emotional support and, in most cases, the child victim is too young to understand the sexual nature of the mother's behavior. She only knows that it makes her mother feel good and she develops strong protective feelings toward the mother. Females are also allowed to engage in physical contact with one another and, therefore, such behavior between mother and daughter is not regarded as incest. As the daughter grows older, she may resent the mother for keeping her emotionally and physically attached by her possessiveness. The full extent of the aftereffects of incest between mother and daughter are not known, but it is believed that the experience results in confusion and anger that can prevent the victim from moving toward healthy relationships in adulthood.

Multiple Incest

In some cases, several family members are involved in incestuous relationships, either simultaneously or sequentially. The most common form of multiple incest occurs when the father is involved with more than one daughter. Incestuous fathers tend to "move on" to a younger daughter when the older one reaches the age when she can free herself from the relationship with her father. After the first incest affair has ended, the father feels less guilty about involving the second daughter and he can initiate sexual relations more easily. Sometimes the older daughter helps her younger sister avoid incest with the father by making the father promise that he won't molest her, but many victims report that their fathers seldom keep their promises.

A second form of multiple incest is combined daughter-sister sexual intercourse with the father and brother. In these families, the father and the brother of the victim engage in sex with her simultaneously or sequentially. Brothers may also join together in sex play with the sister, but it is believed that father-daughter combined with brother-sister is the more frequently observed form of multiple incest. Weinberg describes a family in which this form of incest occurred.[7]

Mr. and Mrs. Peters were married and had four children. Both parents had a meager education. Mr. Peters drank moderately and when faced with a crisis tended to drink rather excessively. The oldest daughter, Louise, started having sexual relations with her father when she was fifteen years old. Her brother saw Louise and her father engaging in sexual intercourse on one occasion and later forced his sister to submit to his advances, giving her money to gain her full cooperation. Although Louise was not adverse to having sex relations with her father, she became resentful when he began to forbid her to associate with boys and placed other restrictions on her behavior. To escape from the father's restrictions, Louise told her mother that he was having intercourse with her.

The daughter's charges against her father created a major disturbance in the family. Louise admitted that she had sex relations with a number of men and that she also had sexual intercourse with her brother several times. When the father learned that the brother also had sex with Louise, he became extremely hostile toward the son, but when she made official charges against both incestuous family members, the situation changed. The brother and father united against Louise to avoid being sent to prison after she confessed to a long list of sexual relations and implicated her father and brother.

As the trial approached, Louise changed her testimony and said that she had lied about her relations with her father and brother. Later, she claimed that she had changed her story because she did not want her father sent to prison, thus depriving the family of his economic support. After the father and brother were freed of the incest charges, the mother denied that the incest had occurred. Family members never discussed the matter because they feared that talking about what had happened would provoke hostility between the father and the brother. The mother was more concerned about having the father freed than about what had happened to her daughter. She said that she had to tolerate the father's behavior because he worked regularly and supported the family. She seemed to overlook the fact that the son had committed incest with his older sister. Louise was sent to a private school for delinquent girls.

In cases of combined father-daughter and brother-sister incest, the female victim is the common partner of her father and her brother. This incestuous relationship creates disorganization and disruption within the family. The father is arrayed against the son and the mother against the daughter. In the end, the mother usually expels the father or the daughter from the family. The daughter is usually the estranged family member because the mother outwardly condones the husband's and son's behavior or because she needs their economic support. Father and son are mutually hostile because they are in competition for the sexual favors of the daughter. Some mothers will not banish either sibling from the home even though they are angry about the disclosure of the incest between the brother and sister. After she has reprimanded the daughter and son, she may return to her routine duties unless the daughter becomes pregnant. If the brother is the aggressor and if the sister did resist his advances, the family may banish him from the home unless they depend on him for economic support.

A third form of multiple incest is intergenerational involvements in which a family member has experienced incest in the family of origin and carries the incest pattern over into the next generation by becoming a participant or by fostering incestuous behavior in other family members. A male who has been exposed to incest as a child may become an incestuous father. A woman who has participated in incest during her childhood may "set up" her own children for incest with the father or other family members. There are several explanations for recreating the incest situation. The mother may be seeking revenge against her own mother who is symbolized in the daughter. Perhaps she is trying to make her husband over into her father's image. The simplest explanation is that women who have been father-daughter incest victims become passive adults who feel that they are helpless against males and can do nothing to prevent the pattern of incest from reoccurring. "Their adult personality characteristics are such that they endure marriages to abusive, alcoholic or psychopathic men, marriages that are conducive to the occurrence of father-daughter incest when the wife withdraws from her sexual role," observes Meiselman.[8]

The Incest Attachment

Some investigators have observed that incest may involve a strong emotional attachment between father and daughter. This erotic bond between the incest participants takes the form of intense jealousy on the part of the father and causes him to isolate the daughter and supervise all of her social activities. In so doing, the father substitutes himself for contacts with other people, especially males, and supresses the daughter's move towards independence. He prevents her from engaging in normal teenage activities, prevents her from attending parties and places a curfew on her evenings. He may even forbid her to associate with girls who he thinks might persuade her to associate with boys or who might encourage her to resist his domination.

If the daughter has a boyfriend, the father tries to disrupt the relationship by disparaging him or demanding that he stay away from the daughter. Or he may try to stop her from marrying by saying that she is too young or is needed at home. Some daughters defy their father and marry despite his disapproval. Others run away from home or elope secretly to escape the father's domination. But there are families in which the daughter reciprocates the father's sexual attention and she tends to regard compliance to her father's sexual demands as a filial function. Eventually, some daughters assume a wifely role as illustrated in the following case.

J.S. was very infatuated with her father. He had fondled her since she was a child, and when she was fourteen he seduced her. They were together on almost all occasions. The father called her "dearie" and she called him "honey." Having never gone with other boys, she had no desire to do so. She was satisfied that her father wanted to be with her and was devoted to her. She, for her part, wanted to be with him. Though the mother knew of their relationship, she feared the father and did not actively oppose the relationship.

If the incest love between brother and sister is reciprocal, the siblings tend to become companions and develop common interests. In some cases, the incest love is so intense that the siblings attempt to marry and legalize their sexual relationship. If the sister is very strongly attached to her brother, he does not seek other women or social contacts. In effect, the sibling incest creates a pseudo-marital relationship, and in some cases, the sisters do marry the brother and remain sexually and socially adjusted in their adult years. Other sisters who have broken off the relationship with the brother and marry are unable to maintain a stable marital relationship. Some become sexually promiscuous or delinquent, but only a few become professional prostitutes.

The sister who cooperates with the brother in an incestuous relation regards him as her boyfriend. In turn, the brother attempts to win her admiration. In the process, the normal relationship between siblings is replaced by an intense emotional and sexual involvement, as in the following case.

In the L. case, the brother and sister were both somewhat shy of companions of the opposite sex. She had a deep affection for the brother since he was the most admired sibling in the family. She designed to accompany him on machine rides when he drove his mother to work. Previously they had relations when the other sister was absent. Though the sister participant was only fifteen years old, she tried to look her best for the brother. The two were constant companions and frequently talked about sex. When they were in the car alone, the sister would kiss the brother and he would "go on from there."

The attachment between siblings may persist even after the sister has married. The brother may try to disrupt his sister's marriage in order to renew the relationship with her without interference from his brother-in-law, as in the following case example of an older sister and her adolescent brother.

When E.C. was three and D.C. was two, they were orphaned by the death of their mother and were separated. E.C. and her brother met again when they were twelve and eleven. They spent two summers together on a farm, and the brother visited his sister every week until he was fifteen. The sister's planned marriage to a doctor was postponed, and she came to the home of her father with a man she had intended to marry, but the father talked her into forsaking this man.

Soon after the sister's return, the son and his sister renewed their familiarity and began to fondle each other and show themselves to be sexually familiar. The sister, as a pretext, would have the brother massage her back. He became aroused and desired her more intensely. A few nights after her arrival, he came to her bed at night and had intercourse with her.

Although they knew that they were brother and sister and that intercourse might be wrong, they were not greatly deterred. The brother became very fond of the sister and wanted to have a child with her. She did not object and soon was pregnant. The brother persuaded his sister to go to a priest and get married. The brother said that he loved his sister more than any girl he ever knew. The sister said that, though she was not deeply in love with her brother, she responded to him because he cared for her so much.

Brother participants who have been separated from their sisters from early childhood usually experience only minimum guilt about the incestuous relationship. Some do not feel intense guilt because of the genuine affection for the sister, but they may be shamed by the social condemnation that they experience once the incestuous relationship is disclosed.

REFERENCES

1. Herman, J., and Hirschman, L.: Father-daughter incest. In U.S. Department of Human Services, *Sexual Abuse of Children.* Washington, D.C., 1980, p. 72.
2. Justice, B., and Justice, R.: *The Broken Taboo.* New York, Human Sciences, 1979, p. 185.
3. Ibid., p. 188.
4. Ibid., p. 203.
5. Weinberg, S.: *Incest Behavior.* New York, Citadel, 1955.
6. Meiselman, K.: *Incest.* San Francisco, Jossey-Bass, 1978, p. 309.
7. Weinberg, *Incest Behavior,* p. 203.
8. Meiselman, *Incest,* p. 330.

Chapter 7

WHAT NEEDS TO BE DONE

> Someday, maybe, there will exist
> a well-informed, well-considered,
> yet fervent conviction that the
> most deadly of all possible sins
> is the mutilation of a child's
> spirit.
>
> Erik H. Erikson

THE important task of protecting children from sexual abuse is not the province of any one professional discipline or any one agency. Nor can any one strategy of intervention solve all the complex problems that are involved in the development and maintenance of incestuous relationships. As the investigation of the extent and nature of incest has advanced, we have become aware that our present resources to meet the needs of sexually exploited youth are far from adequate. We have also discovered that existing institutions unwittingly contribute to the trauma that incest victims and their families experience. Moreover, many of our cultural values and prevailing attitudes tend to encourage or condone the sexual exploitation of children; but there is also evidence that a movement is underway to change our accustomed view of sexual abuse, and we are beginning to develop intelligent ways of intervening when incest is disclosed. Yet much remains to be done. We need to expand and improve existing programs and develop new approaches to treatment. We need to explore the causes of incest by establishing a sound scientific method of research and so discover new information on which we can build in the future.

Coordinating Resources

Researchers and clinicians agree that the development of a comprehensive and effective child-abuse program depends on a well-coordinated system of services. Most communities have not yet achieved this goal. Many programs are piecemeal and uncoordinated efforts that address only one aspect of the problem of child abuse. Some are based on inadequate knowledge of the forms of intervention and a superficial acquaintance with the skills that are essential to helping incest victims and their families. Doctor Suzanne Sgroi points out that "child protective service workers, police investigators, and health and mental health professionals are largely ignorant of the dynamics and mechanisms of child sexual abuse, unaware that they are dealing with a power problem rather than a sexual problem, insensitive to the underlying motivation of the victim's family to suppress the allegation . . . and reluctant to join forces with professionals from other disciplines."[1] Doctor Sgroi suggests that active and coordinated intervention by all professionals working together as a team is the only effective method of combating the sexual abuse of children and adolescents. The essential steps that need to be taken to put such a program into effect include these: (1) creating a group of competent and experienced specialists in child abuse; (2) assigning more than one professional to work with incestuous families; (3) providing for regular review of all cases of sexual abuse; and (4) developing a variety of treatment modalities that can be used to intervene in cases of incest.

To offer services to incest victims and their families, agencies have found that it is advisable to train a few staff members in each agency who will be exclusively assigned to child-sex-abuse cases. Police officers, family service workers, mental health and child-welfare workers who are interested in the problem of incest can be given specialized experience and intensive supervision in the assessment and treatment of incest victims in order to become highly skilled professionals who understand the dynamics of incest and can intervene effectively in providing protection from the victims of sexual abuse. More than one professional helper is usually involved in working with the incestuous family. If the work of these various professionals is coordinated, the service-delivery system will have a better opportunity to operate in the best interest of the abused child. The coordination of these efforts can best take place if there is recognized procedure for the investigation and treatment of all cases of child sexual abuse. For example, there is a clear delineation of the role of the protective service worker as the investigatory agent and a mental health agency that is responsible for the treatment of mental health problems of the victim and the victim's family. The protective service worker not only investigates complaints and supplies information to the mental health worker but is also required to make follow-up visits to assess ongoing protective service needs. In developing a treatment plan, the mental health worker also takes into account adequate protection for the child, the probability that abuse will reoccur, the prognosis for individual family members and the family as a whole, and the mental health of the incest victim. Frequent communication is essential if agencies are to integrate their services. The continuing evaluation of the family's progress is also required, so that if the protection of the child is in jeopardy the therapist can immediately contact the assigned protective service worker to work out a plan that will provide adequate protection. The involvement of a protective service worker can also provide an extra inducement for a family or an offender to remain in treatment.

The use of regular team reviews of child-sex-abuse cases is another effective method of monitoring progress and assessing the effectiveness of treatment. These team-review conferences provide excellent opportunities for discussing the needs of a particular case and for valuable exchanges of information among agencies. Cases can be tracked by review teams to determine their current status, assess progress and suggest changes in the treatment plan. Team review also reduces the feeling of isolation that workers experience when they have no opportunity to share their difficulties and frustrations with other professionals.

Because no one approach is the key to solving incest problems, several different treatment modalities can be developed to increase the effectiveness of a sexual-abuse program. Some workers may become skilled in the use of a particular approach and can join other workers who have skills in a different form of treatment. Family members can then be seen in individual-therapy sessions, while at the same time husbands and wives or mothers and daughters will be treated as dyads. Group therapy can then be used to augment individual therapy and family therapy when indicated.

Educating the Public

Incest is a highly taboo subject, surrounded by mystery and widely misunderstood. "A lot of people don't even know what the word means, and it is going on all the time," said one incest victim. Federal, state and local agencies can take the lead in conducting a public information campaign with special programs aimed at informing children, adolescents and parents about the causes and treatment of sexual abuse. Children must also know where they can turn for help on their own. Posters, billboards and public-service announcements on radio and television can inform children that resources are available and that they do not need to endure incestuous relationships that so often go undetected and untreated.

Parents also need to be informed about sexual abuse. As Sanford points out, "No one can teach a child about the realities of child sexual abuse better than a parent. With whatever personal or societal limitation parents have, they can help the child be a nonvictim because they have the potential to reinforce, answer questions and be continuing sources of strength and information for the child."[2] Many parents are uncomfortable about sexual material and are especially sensitive about discussing sexual abuse with their children. To be informed, therefore, is one of the first responsibilities of the parent in overcoming the obstacles to discussing incest with their children and giving them survival information that will prevent sexual abuse from happening to them. Parents also share a commonly held view that only strangers sexually molest their children and are seldom aware that most child sexual abuse involves family members such as fathers, brothers, uncles, stepfathers and brothers. Therefore, when the child victim tries to give messages that a close family member is engaging in sexual abuse, parents discount the possibility that incest actually has taken place. Parents who have a basis of reliable information will be more apt to give careful attention to the child's complaints and will be more alert to the warning signals that indicate incestuous relations.

Parents also need to be informed about behavior patterns that may subtly lead to incestuous relationships. The behavior of the parents needs to approximate accepted social standards. The behavior must also be consistent with the age of the child's stage of sexual development. Actions that are appropriate at one age may be highly overstimulating at another. Alvin Rosenfeld suggests several guildelines that parents can use in relation to the sexual aspect of the child's development:

1. Parents do not attempt to satisfy their adult genital needs through their children.
2. There is no seduction or overstimulation of the child.
3. There is an ability to tolerate social and personal intimacy between parents and children without actual sexual involvement.
4. Adequate privacy for both parents and children in overt sexual matters, but a willingness on the parents' part to transmit honest sexual information to their children.
5. An ability to change and adapt family practices so that they remain suited to the child's changing age and stage of psychosexual development.
6. A good comfortable relationship between parents and their children.[3]

Parents need to understand the difference between loving sensuality and abusive sexuality when they interact with their children in order to avoid inflicting damage by crossing over the boundary of normal sexual behavior. To achieve this objective, a comprehensive sex education program, beginning with kindergarten and continuing through twelfth grade, is essential to reduce the number of children and adolescents who are sexually abused by family members. Parents should be offered night classes in sex education that stress the positive aspects of sexual expression rather than emphasize the sinful and negative aspects of sexual behavior. Creating a learning environment that encourages questions from students and parents is essential to a successful outcome of these sex education programs. Ignorance permits incest to develop, and secrecy supports incestuous behavior once it has started. Therefore, an enlightened and honest educational approach to the question of how and why incest occurs will help eradicate some of the conditions that have made intra-familial sex a forbidden topic of inquiry and free discussion.

Training Professionals

In-service training and workshops on incest and other forms of child sexual abuse are needed to inform psychiatrists, pediatricians, nurses and paraprofessionals in child-care institutions and programs about the nature and treatment of intra-family sex behavior. Early detection of incest depends upon the ability of these professional persons to identify and detect signs of sexual abuse and initiate intervention to protect the child or adolescent from continued exploitation by a family member. The need for an education program for professionals to make them aware of the nature of incest and to promote early detection is borne out by a study conducted at the University of Oregon Health Service Center. The report issued by Diane Browning and Ms. Bonny Boatman summarizes the attitude of physicians in dealing with incest: "Physicians need to overcome their own denial and become aware of the prevalence of incest. They must be alert to the possibility of incest in high-risk families and may need to overcome their own discomfort and initiate frank, sensitive discussion of the matter with family members. In doing so, they give families a chance to unburden themselves and seek appropriate action."[4]

The study found that only two out of the fourteen cases of incest referred to the center were referred by physicians in spite of the fact that many of these families had had recent contact with doctors. The experience of past incest victims who have consulted psychotherapists indicates that persons in the various helping professions are also reluctant to talk with their clients about sexual relations with the family members during childhood and tend to avoid inquiring into the matter when it is voluntarily revealed by clients. The reluctance of therapists to engage clients in a meaningful discussion of incest is due in part to their own attitudes and discomfort in regard to the incest taboo. Therefore, helping the professional person analyze the difficulty in an objective way can reduce the possibility of giving inadequate attention to the trauma that the client has undergone as an incest victim.

Professionals also need to be informed and knowledgeable about the laws that govern the reporting of incest so that they can follow the procedure set forth in their particular jurisdiction. By reporting all cases that come to their attention, protection of the child from further abuse will be better assured. If no reporting system has been put in place, the professional person can take the lead in pushing for legislation that makes reporting of incest mandatory and provides for investigation of a complaint of sexual abuse by an agency empowered to act in behalf of the child.

Law enforcement agencies are often called upon to intervene in cases of incest, but the personnel employed by the district attorney and the court may not be adequately trained to understand the complex nature of the incestuous relationship and the dynamics of the sex offender. Therefore, an effort to educate them in these areas is of the utmost importance because of the key position they hold in determining the disposition of complaints involving sexual abuse of children. The clinical evaluation of the incest offender is one of the critical aspects of the legal and intervention outcomes of a charge of incest against a family member. In making the evaluation, the risk of the offender repeating the offense and the threat he poses to the victim must be taken into account. Therefore, court personnel need to be aware of the importance of assessing the offender's level of functioning and his overall ability to think rationally and deal with reality. Such issues as the offender's frustration tolerance, characteristic mood, self-image and impulse control must also be taken into consideration.

In making a disposition of the charges against the incest offender, a number of issues need to be examined to determine whether he can be managed on an outpatient basis or whether he requires incarceration or some form of residential treatment. Therefore, the probation officer, the prosecuting attorney and the judge need to have a reliable basis for making the appropriate decision in each case. If the offender is to be treated on an outpatient basis, the court must make this part of the conditions of probation. As Groth points out, the function of the criminal justice system is to provide backup for those who are to provide therapy for the offender.

The authority of the criminal justice system in the form of the court and the probation-parole department must provide backup support for the clinician in such cases. Their help is crucial to insure the continued participation in treatment by the offender until such issues are resolved or, failing that, to provide victim protection by removing the offender from the community. Effective treatment intervention with such clients requires a multidisciplinary and interagency team approach.[5]

Because courts rely heavily on the findings and recommendations of clinicians in making a disposition, psychologists, psychiatrists, social workers and mental health workers need to have special expertise in making an appraisal of the offender. Groth suggests that there are guidelines that can be used in determining whether the offender is a suitable candidate for probation and outpatient treatment. Among these criteria are the following:

1. The incest did not involve physical force or physical harm to the victim.
2. The offense constituted a regression under stress rather than a chronic fixation on children.
3. The offender does not have a prior record of criminal behavior and has not led a criminal life-style.
4. The offender acknowledges responsibility for the offense and is genuinely distressed about his behavior.
5. The offender has dependable social and occupational skills and does not exhibit evidence of major psychopathology.
6. There are strong support services available in the community to protect the child if the father remains with the family.

Professionals who are responsible for ongoing treatment or providing special services for the victim and the family need to be trained in the various treatment modalities that are appropriate to working with incest cases. Those who work with incest victims and their families need to be skilled in the use of crisis intervention techniques at the very outset of intervention. During this stage, the victim and family often require total life support that involves the use of a wide range of community resources to help the family cope with the concrete environmental problems they face and the application of intensive day-to-day guidance in solving the problems that accompany the disclosure of incest. The immediate needs of the family must be addressed quickly and efficiently. In addition, the emotional needs of the victim and the family must also be met. The helping professional must therefore be trained to be highly flexible in approaching the family, keeping in mind the importance of restoring the equilibrium of the family as soon as possible. Short-term therapy follows crisis intervention in order to insure the protection of the victim against further sexual abuse. The techniques involved in these two approaches are different from the traditional methods employed in most mental health settings. Therefore, personnel assigned to incest cases need to receive special training in how crisis intervention and short-term therapy are used to reduce the impact of incest.

Professional persons need to be effective in the use of family therapy as well as crisis intervention and short-term therapy. To be highly adept at using this model of treatment, the therapist needs to be knowledgeable in the family dynamics of incest, including the power structure that prevails in family systems that produce incestuous relationships. Training in the techniques used in changing family relationships and in bringing about a safe environment for the sexually abused victim is essential. The therapist needs to be able to work with the family as a unit as they attempt to discuss the impact of incest, the role reversal that took place, the poor communication patterns and the blurred boundaries between generations. The therapist must also be trained to teach parenting skills and provide a support system that can sustain the family in time of difficulty. Conducting family therapy also requires that the therapist be skillful enough to avoid letting the more powerful family members further victimize the weaker ones. Workshops and continuing-education programs offer special training in family therapy, and in some instances the emphasis is on working with abusing families. More such training programs are needed to meet the demand for social workers and other professional personnel who are skilled in this area of practice.

To undertake to work with incestuous families is a challenging and difficult task that demands great skill. From the outset, the social worker or other professional helper must recognize that many of these families do not voluntarily seek help in coping

with the problem of incest. They often find their way to a social
agency only after some incident comes to public attention indicating that the family fails to meet minimum standards of child
care. Most of these families are either indifferent or hostile to resources of help during the initial phase of treatment. Because of
the resistance that these clients present, they have been labeled as
"unmotivated" and "hard to reach." Therefore, the social worker
takes responsibility for intervening in cases of incest in the interest of the children involved and must reach out to the victim and
the family with a sympathetic understanding that they are having
serious difficulty in coping with their problems. Although the
parents in these families seem to be grossly indifferent to their
children, their resistance to being helped grows out of a feeling
of hopelessness.

The approach to helping these "unmotivated" clients
combines acceptance and firmness and requires respect for the parents as persons without condoning their behavior. Those who have
worked with these "hard-to-reach" clients also have found that a
certain amount of firmness and authority is needed to bring about
change. Professional helpers need to learn how to use authority in
the helping process even though the forced intervention in cases of
incest arouses hostility and guilt. The family may attempt to avoid
dealing with the problem by using denial and by projecting blame
on persons and events outside the family as defenses. These forms
of resistance are to be expected, but as the family begins to realize that the intrusion in their lives is a demonstration of genuine
concern, the resistance begins to diminish.

The traditional methods of intensive psychotherapy are usually ineffective in working with these involuntary clients. Therefore, intervention must focus on the delivery of concrete services
in order to bring about change. Most of these families do not have
either physical or emotional resources in adequate supply and cannot function with any degree of acceptability without the assistance of the community. Social workers have found that they require a wide range of services because they are facing more than
one specific problem. In order to deal with the incest problem,
the family needs help in resolving a host of other pressing and
stressful situations, such as unemployment, physical disabilities

and mental disorders. Therefore, those who are assigned to working with incest cases need to be trained in using problem-solving approaches in social casework and in developing a high level of skill in using outreach techniques. The worker also needs to be skilled in performing the broker role, linking the services of the community to the family's needs, informing the client as to the nature of the services and acting as an advocate who speaks in behalf of the family. The use of the problem-solving approach and the techniques of aggressive casework practice are often effective in producing significant and long-standing change in the life of the family. Workshops and training programs that are specifically designed to train social workers and other helping professionals in methods of practice that are especially adapted to meet the problems of multi-problem families and involuntary clients are urgently needed. Some communities and teaching centers have seen the value in offering such educational programs, but more efforts in this direction would be of great help in training workers who are assigned to cases in which crises intervention, family therapy or outreach casework practice is the treatment of choice.

What Parents Can Do

Although professional personnel can be of help when incest is disclosed, the responsibility for taking measures to prevent the development of incestuous relations rests primarily with parents. Parents need to understand the difference between loving sensuality and abusive sexuality in order to avoid crossing the border between these two forms of parent-child interaction. Clinicians point out that all parents have some erotic feelings and some degree of emotional dependence on their children. Children also have erotic sexual feelings toward the parent of the opposite sex, in addition to the nonsexual ties of affection toward both parents. The erotic and sexual aspect of the parent-child relationship is latent and sometimes buried in the unconscious. Freud pointed out that the sexual and psychologcal development of the individual passes through sequential phases. During the oedipal phase, the daughter has a strong attachment to her father from the ages of about three to six. In this phase in their psychosexual development, little girls try to monopolize their fathers and little boys try to take possession of their mothers. Parents can easily exploit these early erotic feelings of their children and children depend on the parents to set limits on their sexual behavior. To do this, parents must exercise care in avoiding overstimulation of the child by engaging in appropriate behavior.

Few parents who become involved in incestuous relations intentionally set out to seduce their children. Some early experiences, however, may play a significant part in the erotic attachment between parent and child. Most of these experiences involve only incidental contacts that have some sexual content. For example, mothers sometimes experience an erotic response in breast-feeding the infant. Other mothers may touch the infant son's penis. A father may be curious to see or feel the private parts of his daughter and feel guilty about bathing her. Other forms of sexual contact are more harmful. For example, a single mother may take her eldest son to sleep with her even up to the age of ten or twelve. She is unaware that the sexual stimulation of body contact creates problems for the son.

When children reach adolescence, their sexual feelings take on a more adult form and the parent-child interaction is therefore more sexual in nature. Adolescent girls describe two kinds of reactions on the part of their fathers to their daughter's emerging sexuality. Some fathers tend to withdraw and avoid any form of close physical contact with their teenage daughters. Other fathers become seductive or engage in overt forms of erotic behavior, including lingual kissing, explorations of breasts and intimate caressing. Household voyeurism is another form of incidental sexual contact between parent and child. Fathers may secretly watch their daughters undress but believe that it has no impact on them because they are not aware of it.

However, daughters are vulnerable to the father's attention and sexual advances during adolescence. Fathers are also vulnerable during this period because they are subject to the stresses of mid-life and want to feel sexually stimulated and virile. The father can be tempted to exploit the teenage daughter's need for his approval and affection to meet his own sexual and emotional needs. If the father is in control of his behavior, he will recognize that he can inflict emotional damage on his daughter and will refrain from taking advantage of her vulnerability. As Summit and Dryso point out, "A father should be harmless to flirt with. He should be approving, admiring and responsive to her growing sexual attraction and he should provide a controlled, self-limited prototype of the sensual experiences she will develop with other men as an adult." The responsibility for setting limits rests with the father, not the daughter, as the Justices point out.

> Some fathers have no intention of getting sexual with their daughters but are turned on by her acting flirty and seductive, just as her body is beginning to take the shape of a woman. Instead of recognizing the flirtatiousness as the daughter's way to test her emerging identity on the closest and safest male around, he flirts back and responds to it as an invitation for sex. In a healthy relationship, the father doesn't flirt back and doesn't use the child to meet his own needs.[6]

Parents Can Help Themselves

Parents can take steps to prevent the development of incest by learning how to meet their own emotional needs in appropriate adult ways. If sexual and emotional needs are not met by the spouse, the parent is apt to turn to the child for gratification. Clinical studies indicate that incestuous relations between father and daughter grow out of a feeling of alienation between the parents. When the father complains to the daughter about the mother's failure to provide him with affection, he encourages the daughter to fantasize that she can take her mother's place. Mothers who encourage their sons to become the man of the house are also encouraging them to take on the role of lover that involves unconscious sexual strivings on the part of the boy. Therefore, parents who are experiencing problems in their relation as marriage partners need to find a solution that does not place the child or adolescent in an adult role and require children to fulfill adult expectations.

The ability to resolve the marital dissatisfaction requires that the partners communicate effectively in order to arrive at a mutually satisfactory solution. In most cases, the wife needs to ask her husband to provide the kind of positive strokes that are im-

portant to her, and the husband must be able to tell his wife
what positive strokes he requires. Once each partner makes clear
what he or she expects, they can negotiate as to what each is willing to give and what he or she expects to receive in return. The
process of marital bargaining is essentially a *quid pro quo* arrangement that leads to a clear understanding of each partner's needs
and an agreement as to what each partner regards as important
issues in the marriage relationship. If the parents are unable to
undertake this negotiation process on their own, they can ask
for the help of a competent marriage counselor or family therapist
to enable them to communicate and negotiate a contract that will
bring greater satisfaction to both of them.

Studies have shown that a healthy family system is one in
which there is a strong coalition between the parents. If the parents are able to accept each other as equals and have a mutual respect for one another, they can form a strong partnership that
keeps the family healthy and reduces the likelihood of incest.
When the parents are engaged in a continuing struggle for power
and mastery over their partners, the family system is weakened.
Clinicians have found that if the father assumes a dominant position of power in the family the mother begins to feel powerless
and plays a passive-submissive role in the family. Once the father's
position of dominance is established, he can then use his power
to control his daughter and in so doing require her to submit to
his sexual demands without interference from the mother. On the
other hand, if the mother has a strong sense of personal identity
and equality, she can effectively prevent the father from exploiting the daughter. Moreover, if the daughter perceives that the
mother and father are united and that the relationship is satisfactory, she will be less apt to fall into the role of trying to please her
father and make up for deficiencies in the parents' marriage.

· Parents can also help themselves by learning how to avoid
stress. Blair and Rita Justice found that one of the chief causes of
incest appeared to be excessive stress that families undergo when
they make make constant, frequent changes. Any form of change
that requires people to make adjustments makes demands on
them to cope with some different set of circumstances. This demand to adjust produces stress and pressure. People respond to

stress in different ways, but there is an underlying common characteristic: a loss of control over one's physical health, emotional well-being or behavior. Although stress is not a direct cause of incest, it is an important contributing factor insofar as it causes one or more family members to seek a source of relief from pressure. "What excessive change does is to bring out tendencies that otherwise might remain under control," write Blair and Rita Justice. "In some families, excessive change may go on for several years before incest occurs, before a father lets go of the control he normally has over his behavior and turns to his daughter as a sexual source of closeness and comfort."

Blair and Rita Justice suggest that, since excessive change leads to stress that in turn contributes to the development of incest, all families need to be aware that even small changes add to a person's stress. Therefore, they advise that families make only changes that are necessary or will be definitely beneficial once adjustment is completed. The more change that people subject themselves to, the more important it is that they have some areas of their lives that are stable, predictable and comfortable to offset the effects of excessive change. In addition, families need to learn how to keep stress to a manageable level by getting rid of the "language of stress," adopting a new self-care vocabulary and learning relaxation exercises. Learning to manage stress is not, in and of itself, an answer to incest, but it is one factor that parents can be aware of and do something about.

Parents Can Help Their Children

Children who grow up feeling valued develop a sense of self-respect that is a strong deterrent to becoming involved in an incestuous relationship. These children feel good about themselves and believe that they are lovable, competent and worthwhile. Because they have high self-esteem, they do not have to trade access to their bodies to gain affection. The child's parents have a responsibility for instilling his feeling of self-confidence and high self-esteem by offering praise and emotional support balanced with appropriate criticism when the child's behavior merits correction. But most important to a sense of self-worth is the feeling of being loved. Many parents assume that children know they are

loved and that they do not need to tell them. Children often inter-
pret the parent's silence as meaning "I am not lovable" or "Nobody really likes me." Parents who are aware of the child's need
for expressions of affection and approval and who can adequately
meet these needs are effectively reducing the likelihood of incest
taking place.

Parents can also help their children learn to become separate
persons with a sense of territoriality. When the child develops a
sense of territoriality, he has boundaries that no one is allowed to
cross. Therefore, if the child is faced with an unwanted sexual approach, he can use the tools of assertiveness and self-protection to
defend himself against sexual abuse and exploitation. The child
must feel that he is entitled to the same rights as adult family
members. Kissing is an example. Adults know how it feels to be
kissed by someone they want to get away from. But parents
expect children to tolerate this form of intrusion in the name of
affection. When parents realize the importance of territory and privacy, the child can establish distance between himself and others.
This is an important factor in preventing incestuous behavior from
developing. By modeling behavior that exemplifies a consideration
for privacy and distance, parents help the child to achieve his own
sense of self-identity and self-respect.

Parents can also help children to develop friendships with
peers and develop a social network that is a bulwark against the
possibility of incest. Children who have friends are less apt to feel
that only one person likes them and that they must do whatever
that person requires in order to be liked. Making friends is a skill
that is learned, and parents can help their children learn this important skill by encouraging the child to risk possible rejection
and by being available to comfort him when he is rejected. Parents can also serve as a bridge for making friendships with their
children's friends by offering to take them along on a visit to the
zoo or to a baseball game. Clinicians have found that many victims felt isolated and shut off from others during their childhood,
had few friends and experienced severe difficulty in relating
to their peers. Some of the difficulty related directly to the shame
involved in being involved in incest, but the experience of victims
also indicates that the social isolation reinforces the pattern of in-

tra-familial sex. Therefore, as a precaution against incest or other forms of sexual abuse, parents need to be aware of how important a role friendship plays in the normal development of the child.

Parents also need to be aware of the child's need to be a child, not an adult. When parents recognize the importance of letting the child be a child, they do not encourage daughters to make a habit of preparing meals for fathers, mixing them drinks, tidying their rooms or disciplining younger children in the family. Clinical studies indicate that generational boundaries are not maintained in incestuous families. Daughters take on adult roles and responsibilities that normally are performed by mothers. Gradually, the blurred boundaries in the family lead to distorted relationships between the father and his daughter, and the basis for an incestuous relationship is formed. When the mother is employed outside the home, special precautions can be taken to prevent this role reversal from becoming a problem for the family. It is most important for the mother to convey to her daughter that she is not encouraging the role reversal because of her absence from the home, and that she maintain appropriate boundaries between herself and her daughter in all respects.

Parents also need to be aware of the signs and symptoms that incest is occurring and then take steps to remedy the situation that gave rise to the development of the relationship between a parent and a child or between a brother and his sister. Various cues about incest deserve attention, and, while no one sign is conclusive evidence, when one or more are found in combination, incest should be considered as a distinct possibility. The cues that are important indicators can be summarized as follows:

Cues in father-daughter incest

1. Generation lines are blurred, with the father taking the child position and the daughter taking the role of wife and mother.
2. Father acts as suitor to daughter, and mother acts as rival to daughter.
3. Father is overpossessive of daughter and is jealous of her association with peers. Father spends much time alone with daughter and discourages dating.

4. Father shows favoritism toward daughter, and siblings are jealous of the attention the chosen daughter receives from the father.
5. Daughter is depressed, has poor self-image and is withdrawn.
6. Daughter is uninvolved in school activities and may show decline in academic performance.
7. Daughter is secretive, keeps to herself much of the time and has few friends.

The psychological cues listed above are commonly found in cases involving adolescents. Signs of incest in toddlers and younger children are likely to take the form of physical and behavioral manifestations. Among the physical cues are genital irritation, laceration, abrasion or bleeding. Stomachache, painful discharge of urine and veneral disease are also possible indications of sexual abuse. The behavioral cues in small children include enuresis, soiling, hyperactivity, sleep disturbances, fears, learning problems, compulsive masturbation, excessive curiosity about sexual matters and separation anxiety.

Cues in Brother-Sister Incest.

The cues that brother-sister incest is occurring are usually less visible than in cases of father-daughter incest, but these are some indicators:
1. Brother and sister behave as boyfriend and girlfriend.
2. The sister is fearful of being left alone with her brother and avoids him whenever possible.
3. Brother and sister look embarrassed if they are discovered alone, no matter what they are doing.
4. Sister constantly antagonizes her brother, knowing he is unlikely to retaliate for fear she will tell someone about the incest.

Because many victims are reluctant to disclose what is happening, these cues may be indicators that incest is taking place, especially in cases of younger children who do not have sufficient knowledge or vocabulary to talk about sexual abuse. However, parents must take care in jumping to conclusions simply on the basis of any one of these cues.

What Society Can Do

Researchers and clinicians point out that when families are overburdened by stress serious difficulties result in the form of delinquency, behavior disorders, mental illness, alcoholism and child abuse. These families often face numerous environmental problems that have an adverse impact on the lives of adults and children. Families subject to the constant stress of poverty, low income and chronic unemployment are highly vulnerable when they are called upon to cope with overwhelming problems with a minimum of physical and psychological resources at their disposal. Many of these families are hemmed in by ghettos and barrios, live in unsafe neighborhoods and send their children to substandard, poorly staffed schools. Many, if not all of these environmental sources of stress can be eliminated by a serious effort to provide social services — adequate income, decent housing and comprehensive health care.

Unfortunately, our professed belief that the family is the cornerstone of society is not matched by our public policy. We have not really addressed the question of how to guarantee an adequate income or full employment for all families. Existing income supplements to poor families are miserably inadequate and millions of children continue to live in poverty from one generation to the next. As the Carnegie Council on Children points out: "The single most important factor that stacks the deck against tens of millions of American children is poverty. Other things being equal, the best way to ensure that a child has a fair chance at the satisfaction and fulfillments of adult life is to ensure that the child is born into a family with a decent income." There is no indication that poverty in itself is a direct cause of incest. However, there is evidence that poverty is significantly related to poor mental health, family disorganization and other forms of psychopathology. Therefore, the impact of poverty produces conditions that are also associated with incest, namely, disruption of family relationships, low self-esteem and financial stress.

Searching for Answers

Researchers, social scientists and clinicians are engaged in a

continuing effort to find a definitive answer as to why incest occurs. Identifying all the factors that may account for incestuous
behavior is a difficult task because the problem is exceedingly
complicated. However, at least four conditions appear to be involved in the development of incestuous relationships: (1) a
predisposition of the offender to commit incest; (2) a dysfunctional family system; (3) environmental conditions that produce stress;
and (4) cultural patterns that support institutionalized patriarchy.
The combination of these four conditions appears to be present
when incest takes place.

Studies of the personalities of incest perpetrators have resulted
in a clearer understanding of the psychodynamics of incest behavior as an attempt to compensate for feelings of inadequacy and
emotional deprivation. As psychologist Groth observes: "Incest
behavior is sexual behavior in the interest of nonsexual needs. It is
the use of sexual relationships to express a variety of unresolved
problems of unmet needs in the psychology of the offender that
have less to do with sensual pleasure and more to do with com-
petency, adequacy, worth, recognition, validation, status, affili-
ation and identity. It is the sexual misuse of power." In most
cases, incest represents a regression to immature, inappropriate
behavior when the offender is unable to cope with stress or frustration. In cases of father-daughter incest, the offender is drawn
to the child because his relationship to the marriage partner is
unsatisfactory. The daughter is used as a substitute for an adult
to fulfill emotional and sexual needs. Groth has classified these
offenders as falling into two categories: *passive-dependent* men
and *aggressive-dominant* men.[7] Passive-dependent offenders relate
to their wives as a dependent child instead of a competent marriage partner. When their wives do not meet their husbands' expectations for nurturing, these men feel neglected, rejected and depressed. To compensate for feelings of inadequacy and rejection,
these offenders turn to their daughters for comfort and nurturing
as well as for sexual stimulation and gratification. Incest perpetrators who fall into the aggressive-dominant type of male maintain
strict control over their families. They have a strong need to control their wives and children in order to compensate for their
basic feelings of inadequacy. Both the aggressive and the passive

types depend on sexual activity to overcome feelings of helplessness and vulnerability.

However, the predisposition to commit incest does not in itself result in carrying out an incestuous desire. Research indicates that incest is in part a result of family dysfunctioning. Therefore, the search for the causes of incest includes an examination of the disorders in family systems and the psychodynamics of family relationships that are associated with incest. Uniformly, investigators report that incest is only one problem among several problems found in incestuous families and is rarely found in families that are healthy. Studies indicate that incest develops in families when severe disturbances in marital relationships and sexual relationships occur, and that role reversal between mother and daughter is strongly associated with incest between father and daughter. A study by Herman compared incestuous families to nonincestuous families. The comparison led to the discovery of some significant differences between the two.[8] The father was violent in 50 percent of the incestuous families as compared to only 20 percent of the fathers who presented violent behavior in nonincestuous families. Half the informants reported that their fathers were habitually violent and that they had seen their mothers beaten. Other children in the family were also beaten. These findings support the view that fathers who are involved in incest tend to be dominant and aggressive and hold exclusive power over other family members.

The study also supported the thesis that the mother in incestuous families is often physically or mentally unable to fulfill the normal duties of her role. The mother was ill in 55 percent of these families in Herman's study of incest. Depression, alcoholism and psychosis were among the most common causes of the mother's disability. Many of the disorders in mothers went undiagnosed and untreated. The control sample contained only 15 percent of mothers who were ill or disabled, indicating that the mothers in nonincestuous families are, for the most part, able to carry out their role effectively, in contrast to mothers in incestuous families.

The disability of the mother may account for the fact that the daughter played ·a maternal role in 45 percent of the incestuous families and that they played a maternal role in only 5 percent of the nonincestuous families. This finding also supports the view that the reversal of roles between daughter and mother is a significant characteristic of father-daughter incest family relationships. The study showed that over one-third of the daughters in incestuous families had been separated from their mothers for some period of time during childhood because of their mother's disability or because the mother felt that she was unable to cope with the children. This is in sharp contrast to nonincestuous families in which none of the daughters underwent any period of separation from their mothers. None of the informants reported that their parents were happily married in the incestuous family sample, indicating that marital dissatisfaction is a significant factor in the development of father-daughter incest. In many of the incestuous families, the daughter took over the role of the mother and wife. Thirty-two of the forty daughters in the incestuous-family samples were the oldest daughters in the family, and almost half had been pressed into the "little mother" role of caring for younger siblings and becoming their fathers' confidants. This finding supports the thesis that daughters who become involved in incest do so because they feel a responsibility for keeping the family together.

The Herman study is one of few attempts to compare incestuous families to nonincestuous families. Most studies have not included a control group, and more information based on valid comparisons would give greater credence to conclusions about the causes of incest as a family phenomenon. As Schultz points out: "Intensive research efforts are required to determine why most families are not incest genetic. Herein may be the greatest impetus for preventive tactics that can be taught to all families or structured into family and children's policy."[9]

A third condition that contributes to the development of incest appears to be an unusually high level of stress. Men who might not otherwise become involved in an incestuous relationship to their daughters do so when they undergo a period of excessive stress in an effort to offset the discomfort involved in coping with problems that overwhelm them. The study of incestuous families conducted by Blair and Rita Justice provides an interesting and significant finding in regard to the important of stress as a contributing factor in incestuous behavior.[10] Using the Social Readjustment Rating Scale to measure the stress level in a group of sexually abusing families, the authors found that the scores averaged a staggering 240 for these families, representing the amount of change that they had undergone in the 12 months prior to the time when the incest began. In a matched group of nonabusing families, the average score was 124. The authors conclude that stress due to frequent changes in the life of the family is directly associated with the development of incest. The findings also suggest that when the family is called upon to cope with stress, the personal resources of family members are stretched to the limit. Because incestuous families are extremely fragile, the impact of stress and change is highly detrimental.

The fourth contributing factor to the development of father-daughter incest is institutionalized patriarchy in the view of authors who regard the existing family as a form of enslavement of women and their subordination to the power and authority of men. This view is eloquently expressed by Judith Herman:

> The sexual abuse of children is as old as patriarchy itself. Fathers have had sexual relations with their children from time immemorial, and they are likely to do so for a long time to come. As long as fathers dominate their families, they will have the power to make sexual use of their children . . . If incestuous abuse is indeed an inevitable result of patriarchal family structure, then preventing sexual abuse will require a radical transformation of the family.[11]

The transformation, Herman argues, will require that fathers take an active role in the care and nurturing of the young and that the rigid sex roles that are imposed by our existing social norms will have to give way to a more equal distribution of power and authority between the sexes. Herman points out that there is no cross-cultural research that can validate this view or disprove it. Nevertheless, she holds that the greater the domination of the father and the more the caretaking is relegated to the mother, the greater the likelihood of father-daughter incest. "The more democratic the family and the less rigid the sexual division of labor," she writes, "the less likely that fathers will abuse their daughters."[12]

Information gathered by clinicians tends to support the view that the excessive power granted to fathers is indeed a contributing factor in incest. Informants report that their mothers were ineffectual and submissive, had little power and were unable to protect them from the incestuous behavior of the father. A culture that maintains the superior position of men over women indirectly contributes to and sanctions the misuse of power by men and the exploitation of children to meet the needs of fathers in incestous families.

The factors that contribute to incest are schematically represented below, along with the methods of intervention that are appropriate in the treatment of incest.

Strategies of Intervention

Contributing Factor	*Intervention Strategy*
Offender's Predisposition	Individual Therapy Group Therapy Probation Incarceration
Dysfunctional Family System	Divorce Separation Foster Care Family Therapy Marital Therapy
Excessive Stress	Relaxation Therapy Networking Employment Services Mental Health Services Health Care
Patriarchal Family Structure	Consciousness Raising Assertiveness Training Political Action Women's Networks

useful

The effective treatment of incest requires a multidimensional approach in order to effect significant change in the offender, the family or the social institutions that contribute to the development of incest. Therefore, most programs designed to work with victims and their families include a variety of methods of intervention. Individual and group therapy is employed to work with the offender, the victim and individual family members. Family therapy and marital therapy is offered to bring about changes in the relationship between the marriage partners and between the parents and their children. Some programs include training in the use of relaxation techniques to help individual family members cope with stress. Assertiveness training is offered to help mothers and daughters acquire an improved self-image and to restore a sense of personal worth.

Some communities have attempted to evaluate the effectiveness of these various approaches to helping incest victims and their families. Such an evaluation of services was undertaken by the Connecticut Sexual Trauma Treatment Program using a problem-resolution test as a measure of effectiveness.[13] Therapists were requested to identify the problems that were presented in each individual case. The workers assessed each family through the use of a *problem-oriented record* that provided an ongoing record of the family's problems in nine defined areas. As a measure of the effectiveness of treatment, the therapist was required to make judgments as to the status of each identified problem at the point of termination. Each problem was judged to have been resolved, improved, unchanged or worsened. This method of evaluating the outcome of treatment supplied information to determine the effect of the program in resolving problems presented by incestuous families.

The evaluation of services also proved to be useful in revealing the range of problems that the program was called upon to address. The study indicated that family pathology was a major problem in cases of incest. Nine problem areas were identified and the percentage of families having problems in each category was determined. Sexual abuse was clearly not an isolated problem in an otherwise optimally functioning family. All families had internal difficulties in communication, parenting and marital relationships. For a majority of family members, intrapsychic problems that were identified included depression, guilt, poor self-image, low self-esteen, inadequacy and dependency. A majority of the families also presented environmental problems that included difficulty with school, unemployment, adult problems and financial difficulties. Many families also had health problems and were involved in excessive use of alcohol and drugs. The evaluation provided information as to the multiple problems that the staff was called upon to help clients resolve and provided a guide to the need for developing treatment techniques that would serve these clients more effectively.

The prevention of incest lies partly in helping parents learn how to manage stress and how to deal with their own sexuality and the sexuality of their children. The rights of children must be recognized and their protection from sexual abuse and exploitation guaranteed by making incest a reportable offense in order to help them and their families get prompt professional help in dealing with the problem. Measures to strengthen and support the family through full employment and adequate access to health services must be taken in order to provide a safe environment in which children will not be sexually abused. Finally, the prevailing patriarchal family system that places women and children in an inferior position to men must be modifed so as to provide opportunity for the full development of both sexes and guarantee equal status for men and women as partners in the important enterprise of nurturing and caring for the young.

REFERENCES

1. Sgroi. S.: *Handbook of Clinical Intervention in Child Sexual Abuse.* Lexington, Mass., Lexington Books, 1982, p. 578.
2. Sanford, L.: *The Silent Children.* New York, Anchor Press, 1980, p. 220.
3. Rosenfeld, A.: *Sexual Misuse and the Family.* U.S. Dept. of Health and Human Services, Washington, D.C., 1980, p. 94.
4. Browning, D., and Bratman, B.: Children at risk. *Am J Psychiatry, 134:* 69-72, 1977.
5. Groth, A.: The incest offender. In Sgroi, S: *Handbook of Clinical Intervention in Child Sexual Abuse.* Lexington, Mass., Lexington Books, 1982, p. 239.
6. Justice, B., and Justice, R.: *The Broken Taboo.* New York, Human Sciences Press, 1979, p. 217.
7. Groth, *The Incest Offender.*

8. Herman. J.: *Father-Daughter Incest.* Cambridge, Mass., Harvard U. Press, 1981. pp. 169-195.
9. Schultz, L.: Incest policy recommendations. In Schultz, L. (Ed.): *The Sexual Victimology of Youth.* Thomas, Springfield, 1980.
10. Justice and Justice, *The Broken Taboo,* pp. 222-223.
11. Herman, *Father-Daughter Incest,* p. 201.
12. Ibid.
13. Bander, L. et al.: Evaluation of child sexual abuse programs. In Sgroi, S.: *Handbook of Clinical Intervention in Child Sexual Abuse,* Lexington, Mass., Lexington Books, 1982, pp. 345-376.

INDEX

191

Social workers, 173
Sociopathic personality, 37
Stember, C., 120, 136
Stepfathers, incestuous relations with, 14, 90, 99
Stevens, D., 129, 130, 137
Stress, 56-58, 61, 172, 176, 184
Summit, R., 85, 87, 175
Symbiosis, 71

T
Taboos, 10-13
Tormes, Y., 45

U
Uncle-neice incest, 151-153
effects of, 153
University of Oregon, 168

V
Violence, sexual abuse and, 7, 183

W
Walters, D., 26
Weinberg, S., 27, 76, 150, 162
Wells, L., 38, 59

Y
Youth examiners, 128